WITHDRAWN

D0324279

C Out of Soundings

❦ Books by H. M. TOMLINSON. *Out of Soundings—
The Foreshore of England—The Sea and the Jungle—
Waiting for Daylight—All Our Yesterdays—Gifts
of Fortune—Gallions Reach—London River—Tide-
marks—Old Junk*

"... *his eyes are judgment itself*"

Out of Soundings

By H. M. TOMLINSON *with*
Drawings by H. Charles Tomlinson

HARPER & BROTHERS PUBLISHERS
NEW YORK AND LONDON MCMXXXI

Out of Soundings. Copyright, 1931, by
H. M. Tomlinson. Printed in the United States.
*All rights in this book are reserved. It may not be used
for dramatic, motion- or talking-picture purposes without written authorization. Nor may the text or part
thereof be reproduced in any manner whatsoever without permission in writing from Harper & Brothers.*

FIRST EDITION

B-F

PR
6039
O 3508
1931

828
16590

TO JIM

ℂ Contents

₵Illustrations

❡A Brown Owl

One night, the night of my arrival home after a long absence, I was introduced to Joey. It was the first time I had ever looked straight at a large owl, desiring friendship, but wondering whether or not I was going to get it. That owl, sitting on the table, was not a bird. I should call it a gnome. The other members of the family sat round, and laughed. They knew the creature. Evidently he was on intimate terms with them, though there was no laughter in his direct and impish stare at me. His flat face, with its enlarged and challenging eyes, was odd. He stared at me briefly, then turned his head away wearily, as if he had seen all he wanted. I was dismissed. He began larking with those he knew. He walked about with a jaunty and rolling gait, like a sailor who knows what he is expected to do to make people happy. He made them happy. His conduct, in a guise of the utmost gravity, was ridiculous. Presently I tried to join the party. He gave me another stare, and its meaning was plain: You still here? Without warning he flew at me, his grappling hooks in front of him. I drew back, to more laughter; for it appeared that this was his fun.

Joey's plumage is beautiful, though at first

you might not notice it. The beauty of a shadow, with its tones, needs more than a careless glance. This soft swarthiness has regular markings of hazel and buff. When he sits within a greater shadow, his eyes may blaze like orange glow-lamps. Now that he and I know each other he will sit on the back of a chair near me, when I am writing. He shakes his feathers loose, half closes his eyes, and at times makes a contented noise, if spoken to. Or he will come to one's shoulder to sit there, occasionally nibbling round one's ear with his sickle-like beak. But there is no need to worry about that. He knows what his beak can do, but he is a perfect gentleman. His claws can close like a vice, but not on us. It is certain that a bird cannot be a Christian, but the simple truth is that Joey is more like the real thing than most of us try to be. If you offend his dignity certainly he resents it, but he never re-taliates, and he never harbors resentment. He is magnanimous without knowing what that means.

In fact, I think I would sooner write about that owl than about ships or anything else that I may happen to understand in a small measure. He fascinates me because, beyond Freud or Jung, he appears to hint that life is a riddle which we had better give up. No good even dreaming about it?

2

Besides, like the Sphinx, he gives no help, but merely sits looking to futurity with those awful eyes of his.

We have been told W. H. Hudson was afflicted by letters from numerous correspondents who were moved, not so much by the order of his prose, as by the inexplicable behavior of their pets. They supposed that Hudson could guess hidden springs, not mentioned in the manuals, which actuated most animals. Their faith in Hudson's insight is not surprising. I myself once interrupted his meditations with just such a problem; but he was a sceptical man, who well knew the poverty of common observation, and the vanity of human desire which so readily recognizes what naturally it prefers to believe is there. Hudson always coldly directed reason on those pets, and reason is not invariably fair to poor instinct. Yet what he himself could make of the twitching ears of a deer we learned from his enchanted *Hind in Richmond Park*. Let us not marvel over the magic carpet. That would be Axminster, or what not, compared with those ears. They got Hudson to South America and elsewhere, they reminded him of music he had heard as a boy, of inexplicable premonitions he had felt as a man; indeed, those ears persuaded a

3

reader, who watched their nervousness with Hudson's eyes, to believe that their extraordinary movements would presently waft apart the black curtain which hangs between this world and whatever may be on the hither side of it. That is fairly remarkable for a deer in Richmond Park.

We enjoy good stories about animals, but we rarely believe them unless they are our own. Luckily, there is no need to believe a good story before we enjoy it. Those yarns by our neighbours which would have us believe that good morality, noble conduct, subtle intelligence, which are our prerogatives, are at least nascent in humble creatures, are very pleasant, and that is as much as we ought to expect of them. We doubtless conceded more to animals, for reasons we forgot long ago, when we still used totems, than we do now, when natural history is the lesson most enjoyed in the elementary schools of the cities. We knew more about animals before we stuffed them for museums, and even before we had a settled government. The settled government it was, perhaps, that settled it. Our fear of the wilderness diminished. It was no longer necessary for us to watch the outside dark in fear, when we had quite forgotten what could come out of it. It may not be of much importance that we have

grown deaf and blind to the finer communications
from the night, for we get along very well without them now we have our wireless installations.
But there, anyhow, the communications are for
such as Hudson, and for primitives who still live
beside the wild, and even in it, and who may
neglect its signs at their peril. It gave me a chill
once when I spoke at night innocently, but without restraint, of Rimau, the tiger, to some forest
Malays, and saw the embarrassment caused by
my careless ignorance. They did not like it. His
name may not be mentioned. I but wanted some
information, yet it was certain then that they
knew more than they were going to give.

Since then I have enjoyed the good fortune of a
close friendship with this fellow Joey, who is but
a Wood, or English Brown Owl. I do not propose
to tell any tall stories about him, because as there
are not any I should have to make them up; nor
to pursue, biologically, the problems of memory,
joy, love, sorrow, fear, and so on, to their remote
physiological springs in a bird, for I am ignorant
of the way. I could not put that owl's mind, should
it exist, under the microscope. But at least he has
caused me to put my own there for a brief examination, with what result I need not confess.
After all, ignorance, like everything else, is rela-

tive. It is possible that our confidence in our scientific understanding of this broad matter of life cannot be fully justified. Joey is a warning. My assurance fails me under that inscrutable contemplation of his; which is beautiful to see, though there is an element of terror in it, if you dare his glance long enough. It occurs to me while observing him that there may be a ridiculous side to our science, when we are explaining what we know of these lower creatures; creatures quite incapable of forming a systematic and orderly government. An orderly government? We had better be careful, because even with our unique gifts, by which we form complex communities, we should ponder afresh in the neighbourhood of an ant hill or a beehive.

As for this bird Joey, we have examined diligently all the evidence about the Brown Owl in the ornithological textbooks; but I must say that, except for his colouration, and his language— or some of it—and the length of his primaries, and his weight and dimensions, he is still outside those books. He sits above and beyond, beautifully meditative, quietly interested in our strange behaviour, not altogether unwilling to assist us in the careful measuring of his primaries—for we grow more and more concerned with the need to establish beyond cavil his ordinary owlship; but he is outside. He is beyond us. If he knows no more of us than we know of him, then he knows very little.

We at home have seen in him the reason why the ancients chose him as the symbol of learning and wisdom. The reason is obvious enough. It is not because his eyes are deep with shadows, and are better to look at than most eyes; they certainly give, in repose, a hint of mild but austere sagacity. But they seem to tell him, without fail, all he wants to know about anything which takes his interest, and his interest is constant and alert. He has an inspection which begins with an instant and piercing glance, while his body is motionless, and thus he may remain for a full minute, meditating whatever it may be, with a stern fixity which would draw out the innermost secret of a diplomatic note. Satisfied at last that it is worthless, he turns away his head with an expression of tedium, and the object is thus contemptuously dismissed. But that first challenging glance, that night stare of his, though I am used to it, and know that Joey is incapable of treachery, is still somewhat startling when he fixes it on me. You feel like a sinner whose very thoughts are manifest. He sees through you; and thereupon he relaxes, puffs his feathers, and languidly half closes with bluish veils those dark and luminous orbs. But let anything stir in the shadows—I think he can hear a shadow move—and he becomes as tense as a taut spring, and his eyes are judgment itself.

When he sees a matter quite novel to him he has a curious habit of moving his face in a circle; and if the object really excites him, as when he saw his first airplane, then his whole body sways to enlarge the radius of the circle. It is a comic spectacle of eager curiosity, altogether different from his still glance of doom when a mouse is present though unperceived by our crude senses. I used to think that rotary performance of his head was a foolishness of his till once I caught myself shifting my head about to get a name to something nondescript on the floor which glinted in the lamplight. So now I know that when Joey plays that caper he is but obtaining evidence of an object from different angles; he is trying to give it solidity. He could teach any young writer a point or two at that game.

That he reasons things out there can be no doubt. I should rate his intelligence as high as that of a good cat, and his manners and morality much higher. He has a sense of fun. He is very good-natured. Even when badly irritated he never strikes with his full force, but appears to remember in his extreme annoyance just how far his sickle beak may be struck into a hand without drawing blood. Yet it can execute a rat with a single swift puncture through the skull between the ears. The rat has no chance at all. Joey looks very satisfied with himself when he has nailed so big a victim, and evidently expects us to admire him. He lifts his flat intelligent face to us with a new expression of languid and fatuous good-humour; but one foot has the rat's middle in a vice of steel; it would be useless for the unlucky creature to struggle, and it does not. But Joey, I must say, shows no cruel enjoyment, as would a cat, in fooling with his prey. He swoops down and very early dispatches it.

He has never yet shown anger, but only a kind of fierce resentment, which he expresses with a sound which mixes a whistle and a warble, in a high key, his wings outspread and his head held low. And he will do what most cats will not. If he is out after dark, and you call quietly his name into the night, then presently a great noiseless shadow sweeps swiftly at you; and you may be used to him, but control is necessary or you will dodge; and so he alights on your shoulder, nibbles your ear in salutation, and questions you in friendly little undertones. It is amusing to watch a strange cat in its prowl come upon Joey where he is huffed in deep thought on the garden border. The cat sees at once that this is a bird. So near, too. A bird? What a bird! The cat's mingling of desire and fear is plain in its attitude. It would attack, but dare not. Joey does not move, but looks at the trespasser as a constable would at a loafer. The cat slinks off, Joey's haughty glance following it.

One curious trick he has, which, so far as I know, the natural-history books do not record; perhaps because, in the wild, the trick is invariably successful. It is not always easy, by daylight, to pick him out of the shadows of a tree, even when you know he is somewhere there. But if a noisy stranger comes into the garden that owl instantly understudies a dead stump. He elongates stiffly and shuts his eyes; he might be aware that it is his eyes you see first, when looking for him. When he has become a stump of dead wood then he is nothing but that. You may even push him, but he does not relax, nor open his eyes. He is a stump. There is no owl.

He is fond of a bit of fun, but only after dark. Like a cat, he will pounce on small moving ob-

jects. Suppose that you secrete a matchbox, tied to
a length of string, under the tablecloth, Joey
will spy its first effort to get slyly away. However, he looks elsewhere. He pretends that he
has been unobservant. He looks everywhere but
at the suspicious movement. Then, with his odd
walk, that curious rolling gait, like that of a stout
and light-hearted seaman, he strides not directly
towards the movement, but only obliquely, as
though he had just thought of something more
important than play. Yet as soon as he is beside
the object he is on it so quickly with his talons that
there is no getting used to his suddenness. We used
to play this game by moving our hands under the
tablecloth. Now we prefer a matchbox and
string.

There was a time when we thought he had
had enough of us and was about to choose a home
in alien trees. But he remains, and he seems to
have lost his desire for the wild. He keeps close
to the household. He seems to prefer to stay
within sight of the place he knows; for he is a
sociable creature, and at times comes to the window to intimate that he wishes to sit, for a spell,
within the family circle. When admitted he becomes maudlin with his demonstrations of af-
fection, though never servile, like a dog. He

stands no nonsense even when most maudlin. It should be added that he was found, two years ago, an orphaned fledgling. He would have died of starvation but that a youth of the house, who had a way of his own with animals, got a blow-pipe, filled his mouth with milk, and blew it into Joey. The dodge worked. Joey has never forgotten, by the look of it, the one who gave that first kindly attention with a blow-pipe. For the youth has gone overseas, and now Joey sits humped and not at all playful, contemplative, friendly, but by no means inclined to accept me as a substitute for his companion. His particular friend used to be the first to greet him in the morning. Joey came eagerly to the opening of the door. He comes eagerly now, but it is odd to see his sudden relapse into indifference when the familiar sound of that opening door is no longer followed by a sight of the one he most favoured. I thought, once upon a time, that I would like to try my hand at a novel; but that blessed owl is a salutary warning. I know next to nothing even about him, and his share of life's mystery does not amount to much.

There was a memorable occasion when we were visited by Thomas Hardy. I believe that

great man had a special regard for owls; the
author of *The Dynasts*, we may fairly suppose,
would know why the owl is Athene's familiar.
In any case, the venerable poet and Joey unex-
pectedly confronted each other. It was a strange
experience for the rest of us, who stood and
watched them. They did not speak; they regarded each other intently, but I do not know
what passed between them. Presently the poet
turned sadly away; and the owl directed his gaze
elsewhere as though entirely satisfied.

*   *   *   *   *

I had written all that, and I think I had an intention to continue it, perhaps as an attempt at a
purely ornithological study. But a day came when
Joey's young friend returned from overseas. Joey
looked at him and understood, but did not move.
He was not demonstrative, but he began to watch
for the coming and going of his old friend. He
regained his humorous spirit. Then, with surprising suddenness, he deprived me of my one chance
to contribute to ornithology. We stood round him
one morning while he stared at us from the
ground; he was on his back, and that had never
happened before. He stared at us with what ap-

13

❲ Interlude

This time I must go to Switzerland. There was no escape, I was assured. The command to go— it amounted to that—had that note of imbecile frivolity known to every man who is advised by an editor to depart; for it was assumed that I should enjoy the experience, but preferred to pretend, such was my obstinate humour, that I should hate it. What was the reason for the journey? Winter sports. And the Olympic games would not draw me across the road, even for the minute when the international quarter-mile race is being run; though it is true a sprint across a field, without a stop-watch, in an effort to get to a gate before a bull, is well worth watching.

To make a tiresome journey in the hope of fun is one of the strange acts not unusual to man, because, the chances are, anything is better than the mechanical daily round from which the savour has been trampled out. Other animals, when the flavour of their pasturage becomes flat, resort in large herds, we are told, to what are called salt-licks, obeying an elemental impulse. So does man. He must leave his work, and the mere thought of escape inspirits him; he finds pleasure even in elaborate preparations for his escape.

15

But I cannot remember that I ever anticipated the pleasure which the journey itself would afford; now and then you must pack up, and go, and then you can be but watchful, take one thing after another, and hope for the best. Travel is rarely as disagreeable as one had expected to find it. Something is sure to happen to make you laugh at yourself, if not at the time, then later on.

But what an innocent one would be, to hope for the best, when the quest was the sports of other people at a pleasure resort where Teutons, Russians, and Latins were mixed, in central Europe, the time being midwinter! We came at length—my companion was a child, on his first excursion across the Channel—to our destination, a station six thousand feet up, and my small friend was transfixed by the sight of snow, universal snow, and the fact that we must now enter a sleigh. Snow in England, as far as he knew, first was bright promise, but soon was much set about with prohibitions, and then it went. But to use a sleigh, as though it were an omnibus! Here was snow, the true good stuff, deep, dry, and established; that and the stars, so near and large, he told me, was what he had seen in a book. Therefore it was true. That alone was worth the journey to him, a little fact I had not foreseen.

We glided away from the station, or else the station silently retired. There was no noise. We rose above some of the stars; or they may have sunk below us, to shine in lower gulfs of night. What the country was like we could not see, if there were land beyond, and not merely the dark and everlasting void, for our sleigh might have been skirting the rim of the frozen moon, whose surface was dimly white; below us other boreal planets were shining. I did not ask myself now whether it was likely that winter sports were enjoyable. I was wondering whether I could keep warm enough to hang on in outer space for the chance of sunrise. The transition is swift, from an overheated Swiss railway carriage to a glacial exposure amid the constellations.

We came to the porch of a hotel. It was not reassuring. There we found a group of young Englishmen—in those circumstances, the group would be of that sort—and they were cumbered with ski and outlandish gear. They were very happy. They even spoke to us. Their gaiety, in that place, showed their nationality, for they looked like the forlorn hope of an Arctic search party, and that would make any Englishman feel that life had something to be said for it. Here again my sole reward, so far, was the demeanour

17

of my small companion; he showed that he felt he also was seeing life as it should be. Here he was, at last near the real thing. He heard, as I did, those young men praising God because of plentiful snow and a low temperature. Somebody, too, had broken his leg that morning.

We arrived at that eyrie after dark, so a suspicion was natural next morning that we were far above the earth. I opened the bedroom window-shutters in curiosity, desiring to learn by daylight how far in space we were from home. We might want to get back, some day.

We were nearer than I had thought. Two firs, their dark arms holding out as much snow as they could carry, stood just outside, but nothing else was outside; beyond them was emptiness. Though they were something. There was not a sound in the void, till some unseen children laughed in it; and there is no doubt that a more reassuring base for one's doubtful hold on things than the laughter of children would be hard to get.

The light improved. Across the emptiness, which was a valley, to which I could see no bottom, a dark forest mounted steeply into a white blur that merged into a pale sky. At times I could see a spectral dance up there in the sky, a commotion in the vague clouds, and presently through a parting of them appeared a superior and baseless mountain peak, remote and bright in a morning sun which could not see us. That peak was translucent; it could not be gneiss and schist; it was nothing material; it was only the apparition of what is beyond and not for us. As I looked at that peak, and saw others appear, with glaciers, in a lofty dawn, I came to the prompt conclusion that there would be no ski for me; not any of that tomfoolery. I was there on business.

One glance round the breakfast-room told me that nobody else was there on business, not on business relevant to those harsh economic laws by which we either survive or do not. Perhaps the morning light affected us. London had been drab for months, and I myself felt the gay impropriety of the novel radiance. The very people who at home are so careful to make the correct appearance, at all times, that they can be offensive to inferiors and the thoughtless, here dressed in a way which left one free to do as one pleased. One young lady had a hat which Cruikshank designed for Bill Sikes, a reefer jacket, black pantaloons and puttees, and a pair of boots borrowed from a navvy, by the look of them. Somewhat later that morning I saw her flying down a de-

scent of snow, and then it was another matter.
She would have overtaken Diana, going thus.

And what, asked my small companion largely,
are we going to do?

Nothing! Well, just walk about, and see
things.

Nothing? It must have been the new kind of
light, and those skaters on the rink below, meteors
with intersecting orbits of scarlet, emerald, and
gold, in a white expanse. The rink? The snow
run? I ruled out ski-joring, after an episode I
had witnessed in the village street just before
breakfast. Not that. For a matronly person, severe and large, and wearing ski, the conventional
cap of a burglar, and in other raiment not out of
accord with her cap, provided herself, before my
eyes, with a handle-bar. To this was attached a
trace, and the trace was attached to a horse. The
horse had bells on its scarlet collar. A man
mounted the horse, and off all went, very grace-
fully, to the music of the bells. It ought to have
been applauded.

But the street of that Alpine hamlet, in its
abrupt turns, was only as if it had been thrown
anyhow on the slope, and as the horse attached to
the lady reached the first corner it met a German
gentleman. In addition to his less noteworthy

apparel he wore a vivid green hat and a long
beard; the horse was unprepared for it. It reared
in amazement. Then it turned on its track as if
to question the lady following as to the motive
of this German. Its sudden movement confused
the trace with the lady's ski, and the horse, still
more surprised, backed swiftly from a flash of
reversed black legs with long upper slats.

No, not ski-joring, when a horse could never
tell what it would meet round the next corner.
But we must do something. What should we do?
I had learned already that this valley was a possible cure for dummification of the mind. It
seemed to me that all the languages of Europe
were spoken at our hotel, except Icelandic, maybe.
It had a porter who could answer any question
in one's own pure dialect, whether of Cork or
Catania, and he explained to me that this was
because he used to clean boots in Bloomsbury. I
could never fully believe that he was only a porter; in his uniform, he could have passed for a
surprisingly well-read general of a romantic continental state. It struck me that he must be of
London birth until he turned to instruct a Russian in the local postal arrangements, and then
advised some little children from Palermo where
to find the luge.

The luge! Nor did I want the luge. And skating was insufficient; it was worse than insufficient, because I dared not venture on an intersection of those coloured meteors in their orbits. That day the two of us merely observed the sunlight on icicles and snow-laden trees. But in the evening the Tempter appeared; he was dressed as an English youth and spoke in the Oxford way. "Do you ski?" he asked me.

"No," I told him; "but if he wanted a hand at cards . . ."

He did not. Why was I there? He spoke of high altitudes, from which could be seen all the kingdoms of earth, down to which one flew, secure in the air, turning from peril with the indifference of a swallow. The very next morning was in gold, with snow in the innocence of its original precipitation, bright as an early birthday. I saw it, and remembered the talk of that young man of the night before, when idling past a shop, outside which stood ski and mountaineering apparatus. I paused too long; I went in.

A man inside led me to a stack of ski, and told me to reach to the top of a pair. I could just place my hand on the up-ended prow of one of these narrow boards. The right length! The right length to me seemed an enormity, but I was led outside, and the man strapped the planks to my feet, handed two sticks to me, and departed.

My elation had gone. I was strapped to the road. I had a firm conviction that I should be like the marble drinking-fountain close by, a permanent feature of that village street; the next day visitors would come up to inspect me, snow on my contours, and would look for an inscription to see what I commemorated.

Then one ski began to move. We will call him Castor. Pollux remained firm for a moment, then saw that Castor was leaving him, and followed in haste. My feet no longer were in my charge. They were controlled by twin spirits, who were friendly and sportive together, for they had come to a secret and sinister understanding about me. I could never guess what they had agreed upon, though sure it was no good to me. Sometimes I divined instantly what the end of a bit of devilment would be, but while I was frustrating that manœuvre they deviated.

And another thing. It was the amiability of those twins which were most to be feared. Their really diabolical plots were hatched when, my mind growing easier about it all, I felt I had got them tamely under my feet. It was with that sudden sweet surrender that they took me nicely

23

down the road. I had got them going. This was easy. This was good. They were running in docility side by side, well under control, when there was an explosion of sleigh bells behind me, and a brawling, in Magyar it seemed to me. I turned to enquire, and saw over my head the plumed manes and foaming mouths of two black horses; and at that instant my ski took root in the earth. They were trees again. The sleigh brushed me as it shot past, and the temperature of that Alpine winter became tropical in a flush.

As soon as the sleigh had gone my ski came off the ground, and I was free again. I cajoled the pair with wheedling tact, because now we were some distance from the hotel, and the way home was uphill. Would they go uphill? I did not want to consider the problem of return, for it was easier to go downhill, and that was problem enough. Somehow, Castor and Pollux were persuaded to allow me to reach the verge of a snow field, away from the road, and not so open to observers.

The snow was a long slope, and to the eye was of smooth and gentle design. The view was superb. On one side were high peaks with glaciers glistening in the sun, and elsewhere rose the austere summits of Roseg and Bernina, white above their forests. The snow before me un-

"*. . . but I could not see beyond the footpath*"

dulated down to a footpath, and beyond the footpath—but I could not see beyond the footpath. From my vantage, the empty air was on the far side of it.

Fear seized me. But it was impossible to stand there, pretending to admire the view. As would a man of his word, I commanded the twins to go. They went. I left this earth. Which of the nebulæ would I strike? But it was not for me to choose which. The wind poured past with a voice like the murmur of an organ. The snow fled under us with the spin of the globe, and a forest was coming up to meet us. The prows of my winged shoes smoked like comets. If they were heading for Orion I could do nothing to help them. My thoughts flew in and out—I left them behind . . . there rushed up the last white rim of my own planet, which now I must leave. I reached down with a stick to give a last farewell touch to earth; and then, as a novel would tell us, all went dark.

Somewhat later I found my mouth was full of snow; my head came out of a hole it had made in something. The horrified eyes of my small companion, who had followed me on a toboggan, met mine, and he said, "Are you all right?"

I was. I would try again. But Castor and Pol-

lux were locked in an embrace, out of sight, in a
snowdrift. They moved in an ecstasy of mirth,
and for a time paid no attention to me. But would
it be right to expect the shoes of Hermes to act
as though they were goloshes? What is winged
will fly, and if you do not care for flights through
the light of morning, then you should not put
pinions to your feet.

❪ Gilolo

That island had always attracted me, in the way a fabulous sea-desert does a reader who is over-fond of *Robinson Crusoe*. Yet my island is more secluded than Crusoe's; though it is a geographical fact, that is all it is. A book about it does not exist, to my knowledge—there may be one in Dutch—and my chance of ever seeing it as a landfall was as remote as are the Hesperides from us all. Now and again I chanced on its name in a traveller's tale, though the reference was never more substantial than a bare allusion; my island acquired merely the deepened attraction of what is withheld. There is, as you know, a plentiful bibliography, scientific, of the imagination, and even of the department of humour, built on its next big neighbour to the eastward, Papua: but I have met with only one authority on the subject of Halmaheira, or Gilolo, and that young man, of Holland, who had been exiled upon the island, and when I met him had but just escaped from it, was too reduced by fever, and so unused to the society of his fellows, that he never said anything about Gilolo except "it is not good."

Look at it on the right chart!—but no, you had better not. You will be lost, if you get hold of the kind of chart a sailor must use when approaching it. That island is an ample place; the equator divides it; the blank spaces of its chart and the warnings to mariners show that you might die there if your experience and intelligence proved to be inadequate; the names scattered about its coast would draw anyone half round the world, which is the exact distance of the island from skyscrapers and the fun of the fair; its coast line is so devious and convoluted that to sail round it would be a long adventure, with never a warning of what to expect up that river or round that cape. We had better leave its chart alone.

A day came, and sunrise was the time, when at last there dead ahead of me was the very island itself. I was halfway round the world. The island was as unreal as ever; it was only a lower shape among the vapours of dawn. Before we neared it my ship landed me at another and a much smaller island of the Moluccas, where Drake was entertained by the Sultan. There I had to stay, though that was no hardship. Across the water, from the beach of Ternate, every day I saw the fantastic cloud of Gilolo still persisted on the sea, and merely changed its colours with the hours. But as for crossing over to it, who would put out to land on a cloud?

A Dutch medical officer, while taking his gin
and bitters, said to me, in extreme displeasure,
that he was soon to visit Gilolo. It was most
lonely. He was not a sailor, he was a soldier. The
garrison over the water, it was necessary to visit,
very bad fever and yaws, also dysenteries. He
would be pleased if I go. And that was why I
went down to the jetty of Ternate, early one
morning, and found indeed the official motor-
launch, with two Malays squatting on its bottom
boards. The voyage to my island began to appear
so easy a probability that my scepticism hardened.
For one thing, the doctor had not arrived. It was
hardly time for him yet, maybe; still much too
early for an official. As for me, already the power
of the sun made me feel that even Gilolo could
wait a little longer; or even for ever, now the
inducement was immediate. When we may, we
do not. If the doctor did not come, then I could
stay where I was, and not repine. One of the Malays invited me to take a seat in the launch, but
its space was cramped and it was too glaringly
white and hot. The big island over the water was
a violet chimera with a notched back. Mr.
O'Keefe was near me on the jetty, talking freely
to the crew of a prahu; I saluted, and made to

approach that Irishman, but he only scowled and turned away.

I had to wait alone. It was the Dutch padre who had introduced me to Mr. O'Keefe, the night before, and because I had shown some doubt about him; for this missionary had informed me that he had christened, only last Sunday, three black children of an Englishwoman who lived on Gilolo. He was trying to persuade me that my unexplored island was already infected by civility. I assured him that these exiled and outlawed countrymen of mine, whenever I had met them, were no more like English than Kalmucks. If they spoke English, it was only a Suez variety of the language of sailors. "All right. You come with me and see Mr. O'Keefe. He is English." It was useless to warn a Dutchman that O'Keefe, should he prove true to form, might try to kill any man who called him English. So we went to see this Irishman, who owns an island in these seas, and cultivates coconuts. Mrs. O'Keefe, too, was there. It was night; there was an oil-lamp that was no better than a symbol in a dark temple, and in that gloom the Irishman's wife might have been a dubious pagan deity posed in seclusion. With her feet tucked under her on the floor she sat with a hand stretched on each knee, looked down her

One swarm of them, glittering like a constellation before the dark opening of a cave, suddenly dispersed in minute flashes of blue lightning. Another cluster were of saffron with black stripes, and they were swaying in a draught I could not feel up above; they slowly dissolved, and then reappeared to sway elsewhere. I was only looking on; in the heat of the day the sight was the only sense which kept awake. An array of shining torpedoes swept into the transparency, and the little flowers vanished. The glass below me trembled, the bottom of the sea wavered, reticulated, and faded. Now I could see its surface.

"We go now." I looked up, and the young doctor was behind me, smiling, his raiment white from boots to helmet, and with him was a Malay carrying a leather case. We embarked. Soon we were in the rip of the tide. The native at the wheel touched the gear as a skilled instrumentalist, and the way he chewed betel should have given the doctor full confidence, but the doctor confided to me, "I do not like this." A younger Malay squatted in the bows, on the lookout, with about as much movement as a bronze figurehead. The engine crooned a song to itself, which varied in its loudness as she rolled, lifted, and plunged. I looked astern, and the jetty had shrunk into the

". . . *a diminishing array of miles of pale
coconut palms*"

high bulk of Ternate. The fleet of canoes of the fishermen had partly melted and were indeterminate in a glare. We opened out the shore, which was marked by a diminishing array of miles of pale coconut palms. Those palms were the sea-verge of the precipitous green forest of the volcano which was our home. Now we could watch, not without suspicion, our island's head, far, rufous, and indolently puffing its smoke.

The launch rolled and toiled along, but Gilolo came no nearer. I thought it had receded. Its accessibility, with a ship as small as ours, was not apparent. The sea, too, was by no means as placid as it had looked from the jetty. It behaved in a way that was curious to me; but then its bottom was unequal with reefs, and no doubt tides and currents could be at a serious difference in that channel. The waters swirled and upheaved unreasonably.

The mountains of Gilolo appeared to have heightened; but then, I had to remember we were down among the waves. That array of gigantic shapes, high and acute, could have been on one plane and without body, all equally distant, for they were without shadows. Gilolo was but an illusion of land, the theatrical back cloth for a drama without human attributes. Our little boat swayed and cheerfully sang in the sun, and that was the only sound, and for I do not know how long.

I noticed, presently, that those distant heights were acquiring bulk. Shadows fell between the ranges. The straight line of coast developed bays, and began to emerge as promontories. One gulf retired gradually, as we progressed, to a surprising penetration of the island. Gilolo grew more vivid, and its colour was green, though without the least variation. It was a toneless green, from the shore to the sharp peaks, for it was all forest, all unexplored forest. What work, to learn what was among those mountains! Not even a canoe was on this side of the strait. It was strange that our little craft should make so cheerful and innocently impudent a noise when approaching that immense silence.

No beach was to be seen. The forest rose from the water, as steep as cliffs of emerald. I failed to see how even yaws could be found there. We stood in, and two arms of the island unfolded to meet us, and between them we went, and on the port side turned to a landing-place and a few huts. Nobody met us. We landed, and went along a track towards a huddle of shacks abandoned to silence, under a scatter of lofty palms; when we

38

reached them, a few nocturnal and melancholy
women, who separated from the shadows when
they moved, glanced briefly and sadly at us. Perhaps they knew that our brisk interruption from
the world of men could not break the spell of
their place. The doctor entered a larger hut, and
left me to please myself. I could do nothing to
help him, his business being what it was.

In Gilolo the sounds of life had not begun. It
was broad day, and therefore I knew the island
was not sunk in the sleep of midnight. A dog or
a child would have increased a wayfarer's confidence. My steps made a startling uproar among
leaf parchments on my way to the mangroves;
the harsh noise made me turn to the huts, to see
whether my indiscretion was signalled. Their
faces were blank. Nothing living was in sight.
My friend the doctor was swallowed by the quiet.
When out of sight of the settlement, eruptions
of grasshoppers went before me in the herbage,
and made a continuous whispering, parched and
secretive. Not even a butterfly was there, and usually one does see at least that in a tropical wilderness, to give a touch of original joy to an outlandish place. Once, though, I heard a sweet and
plaintive trilling in a shrub, like that of a warbler, and it was then as if the primeval nature

of Gilolo stirred with the origin of a known life.
I did not hear it again. But it fortified me when
I was down by the black mud of the mangroves,
where the prospect belonged to an earlier geo-
logical age, and thousands of hermit crabs strolled
about the slime with their shells over them, as
bonnets. I did not see the labyrinthodont, the
monster that once frequented such a scene when
coal was a flourishing forest of the prime, long
before it was near being merely one of man's economic problems. Yet though the appearance of
that autochthonous reptile, upheaving from the
morass, would have been proper to Gilolo's mangrove swamp, I was prepared for him, for I had
heard a warbler beforehand, and so was sure I
was in my own day, and not his. For the same
reason, too, the crabs were amusing; the shells
they carried awkwardly about made comic wob-
bling movements when they hurried, like the in-
secure bonnets of old ladies all desperately eager
to catch a bus. When I looked up, the forest across
the creek regarded me with the large composure
of a guardian of the unrevealed, confident that I
should attempt there nothing that was foolish. It
knew that its aspect was sufficiently repressive.
(But ah! if one had only more time! To have

gone over, and entered that forest, and continued
to its Pacific shore!)

The doctor appeared again. The chanting of
the boat's motor on the way home brought a smile
of relief to my companion's face, but it did not
alter the countenance of Gilolo, which stood over
us darkly, to watch us depart. We got out of its
arms, and were at sea again. Now, it was our intention to have a meal in the boat, on the home
run, but its behaviour was discouraging. A serious
dispute developed between the seas and the sub-
merged reefs, and our launch was involved in it.
The seas were angry, for they were in a hurry,
but were checked. The doctor turned hopefully
to look at our own island, to see how near it was.
But it was not near. It was no sort of home, at
that distance. It was only a cone, resting on the
horizon. The boat jumped, then wallowed in a
trough, and a gallon of water fell at the surgeon's
feet. We had no deck.

We worked more into the open, and there the
turmoil of malignant seas forming pyramids and
toppling ridges obscured the shore for which we
were making. Our motorboat became smaller, I
thought. Its movements now were unpredictable,
and I must confess to an effort to confirm my
faith in an engine which, I was glad to see, was

made at Southampton, for if that broke down through stress, unless something worse happened we should have to drift under the sun next day for nobody could say how long, and without water. Even a brave man might not choose to be adrift at sea in that unfrequented low latitude.

A comber exploded, and the engine raced. The poor doctor's face went grey. He was drenched. His English was scanty, but he found some then, and exclaimed in simple candour, "I am afraid." I was anxious myself, though not yet afraid, for I had been watching, in suspicious curiosity, our Malay at the wheel. He knew what he was about. No man could have handled that craft better than he. He parried the attacks like a clever fencer. Besides, was it not unthinkable that an Englishman should be drowned with a Dutchman and three Malays in an unimportant channel of the Moluccas? Of course it was.

We sighted a large sailing prahu, and overhauled it rapidly. It was steering an erratic course, and this puzzled our Malays, who made over to determine whatever might be wrong. We drew alongside, and saw she was abandoned, though she was dry and shipshape. Our men manœuvred the launch, against the violent orders of their superior officer, in an effort to get a line and a

man aboard the derelict. The spray smothered
us again, but here was a really serious matter at
last, and the Malays calmly ignored the doctor
and his expostulations. A youth hung overside on
his toes, and made fast. Away we went, after an
alarming confusion of many bumps and clamor-
ous fountains, with our tow. Did a doctor for
soldiers foolishly imagine that Malay seamen
were going to give a perfectly sound prahu to
the wastes? The prahu with its outrigger foamed
astern, and I was expected to watch the tow-rope.
In another hour we were under the comforting lee of our volcano. Gilolo was an illusion
again; its fantastic ramparts had darkened to pur-
ple under a sunset sky of rose and cinnabar.

The sea between us and Gilolo was a floor of
transient opalescence. When that light went out,
so did the sea, except a phosphorescent glowing
in the foam from our launch and its tow. It
was night; but the peak of Ternate, in the meridian, was either active, or else a belated hour of
day was caught on its rim. Red clouds or fiery
smoke stretched from the crater as luminous pen-
nants. Within the dark between the palms along
the shore points of light were sprinkled. We
could hear voices on the beach.

43

⁋The Turn of the Tide

At the lowest of the ebb of a spring tide, just
where the smooth sands of Burra are so saturated
that their polish inverts the sky, and on a day
when a flat sea makes no division between land
and water, some dark hummocks appear. They
are not uncovered except at low water of a spring
tide, but then they are plain, though of no height;
that dark area in the miles of shining and im-
maculate strand is then as notable as would be a
ship ashore.

Visitors seldom trouble to go down to see what
the nondescript markings are. It is too far. They
keep to the ridge of blue-grey boulders which
protects the land from the breakers of storms.
From those boulders to the sea is a long descent
into vacancy, when the tide is out, even on a fair
day of summer. It is too far down into an empty
but brilliant world. The people who are making
holiday keep to the ridge, which shelters the village; it is easier and more natural to stroll the
other way, down the hither side of the boulders,
and up the street, to the shops and houses and
the assurance to be had from seeing other people
about. There is nothing to windward but the
glinting of the Atlantic.

When we were young it surprised us to see that distant blemish on the polish of the sands at low water. What was it? It was as though the sea had left one of its secrets ashore, in daylight; though whether it was in the water or really at the edge of the beach, it was impossible to say. It was a flaw in a mirror. Yet nobody appeared to notice it. Nobody was curious. Nobody suggested an exploration. And certainly it was strange and a little fearful, all that air and light seaward. It was vast and bright and without sound, and perhaps we were better off where we were, on the boulders, which were solid and heavy, with much that was curious secreted in their damp crevices. Out beyond our foothold the world did not seem real nor safe; so much space, and so shimmering a brightness. Even the sands were shining, and shivered in a breeze, like the skin of a bubble. If we trod on it, that bubble might burst, and down we should go to the clouds, which we could see floated below the beach as well as above it. Out there the air quivered. That world was too far and bright to be safe. It did not look like the earth at all, but only the wide silence beyond the earth. If a wave moved in, it was only a brief shadow, it broke, and you could not hear it. It only glittered

". . . and up the street to the shops and houses"

The black markings, when we reached them, appeared to be of no importance at all. We had come to a patch of tough and darkened clay. The sea had smoothed it, rounded its corners, varnished it here and there with a green glaze. It was pitted with the holes of a boring shellfish. We saw the white shells in places, sticking out from holes like double razors. Rills and gushes of the tide made islands of these hummocks, and between them were deep pools. It was a curious place, exposed and lonely, and the pools were alive with shrimps. In one tank of glass a cuttle-fish, just as we arrived, shot through it like a gleam of blue light. He vanished somehow, though we could not see where he had gone; he had spread among the vague colours at the deep bottom of the pool. But while we were still trying to find him we noticed what we thought was a black leg-bone sticking from the clay by the edge of the water. We tried to get it out, but it was brittle, and snapped. It was not a bone, but a root of a tree. What was a root doing there? Then we saw the clay was full of black bones. On its wet surface the roots coiled about, as they do in life, which was very puzzling, for how could they have grown there? The clay was full of roots.

49

So our first guess, that a tree afloat had foundered there years ago, would not account for it. We took our spades, and dug into it, and then found we could part the stiff black paste into layers, as thin as paper, for it was like a mass of pressed leaves. It was of leaves. We found the familiar outline of an oak leaf, just as one does in the old soil in the shadow of a wood. While wondering over that, pulling a lump of the rubbish to pieces to see what was inside it, we found a hard round object—why, of course, though it might have been a carving in ebony, it was a hazel nut! Had all this stuff grown where we saw it?

We looked back to the ridge of boulders. It was a mile away. It was too distant to make out anyone on it, or even what it was. Only the old church tower on the hill behind it was recognisable, and the houses. There was no forest, we knew, for many miles inland. Then the first impulse of the returning tide sent thin layers of water in arcs up to our feet. The pool with the cuttlefish became agitated and thick with sand. Nothing like a forest was near us. The water was becoming noisy. It was time to go.

What did this discovery mean? Leaves and nuts and shellfish, yet the sea which drove us away!

How could such things be together? Oak-roots
and a cuttlefish! Things had got mixed. The sea
was where the land used to be.

We did not talk about it on our return journey
to the rock and our friends. It is not easy to understand, when you begin to see that the sea and
the land can change places. How long does it
take? Does it take more than a lifetime? The
queer shimmering of the wet sands before us in
wind and light helped the suggestion that the
earth was not so solid as we had thought it, and
that strange things could happen, and nobody
know it. I remember that our elders were not very
interested in our discovery. They were talking
of other things. What was this old forest? There
were no hummocks to be seen then. The tide was
rolling over them, in so short a while. We might
have been mistaken; but I had the hazel nut in
my pocket, though that was not much to show
for so great a change. Our elders, in fact, were
talking of a piece of good fortune which had
come to somebody. It concerned that field behind
the rocks on which we were sitting. It had been
bought, that field, for next to nothing. Somebody had got it and was going to build a house
there. Could there be a better place? An excellent site, somebody remarked. So near to the

beach, and sheltered from the wind. Its value would increase as this secluded little hamlet became better known, as it deserved to be.

How long ago was that morning? It does not seem long ago. That hazel nut still survives, and as I look at it on my desk I can see the wet sand darkening round our feet, as we walk in the sun. As who walk? Where are the people who sunned themselves that day on the rocks? They all cannot meet again. When last year I was on those rocks, in a glance the world appeared as it did yesterday, or years ago. There were the hummocks. The boulders were in place. That light out beyond might have been the eternal light; it had not ceased to quiver, as though alive and immortal, and even the gull reappeared, in a flash, as I watched. Perhaps the ridge of boulders did not seem to be as high as when we first knew it, but there could be more than one reason for that.

Yes, our memory was at fault. When I looked round, there was the scene which had given us, long ago, the happiness of abiding tranquillity. That immense gulf of brightness assured us still of a changeless and radiant peace. The clouds were the same clouds. Those waves, advancing in leisurely ranks, falling along the strand in deliberation, were the same waves. The transient arcs of thin glass, rimmed with foam which the tide impelled over the sands, were so familiar that they could have been there all the time, more lasting than the works of men.

"Well," said my companion, "then this will be the field which some one was lucky enough to buy. Must be, I think. There was no other."

Yes, it was the field, what was left of it. Whoever the man was, he had built his house, but it was the worse for the weather. He had ceased to live in it. When? He had made a garden, but the ridge of boulders had invaded it. Rocks were scattered before his dilapidated porch. The tops of the garden pales projected, in places, only just above the stones. The invasion was real and deep; part of the roof of the house was blown awry.

There could be no doubt about it. This was the place. There used to be a row of cottages opposite that field, with a path between; and there they were still, though changed. The path was not to be seen. Boulders filled the end of the little street which had been kept so neat. The row of cottages had shrunk, but I could not guess by how much. At the seaward end of the row the dead turf of old gardens was hanging from a little cliff of

53

That quaint and pious narrative by Fletcher of
Drake's circumnavigation of the globe, with its
occasional rustic levity when the stealing of Spanish property has to be recorded, is a tantalizing
document. Fletcher was "Preacher in this im-
ployment," and he carefully counts the coins
when a Spaniard is lightened of his purse, and
then dismisses the wretch with a genial reminder
of his good fortune in having fallen into kindly
hands. This is attractive; it gives us a clear peep
at Parson Fletcher. He is hearty, but in our day he
might be thought loutish; the other wonders of
the voyage, not quite so accountable as prize-
money, did not always win his close regard, and
his record therefore is often childish and idle
just when we are most curious. It is easier to
deduce Fletcher from *The World Encompassed*
than Drake. Here and there during the voyage a
reader grows a little impatient; for the time came
when the ship entered the labyrinth of the islands
we call Indonesia. Those islands were at the
end of the earth to Tudor seamen, and hardly
more authentic than a fascinating invention, yet
Fletcher reports little more than unidentifiable
scraps about that region. Tired, maybe, of the

long voyage, he appears to have been as incuri-
ous, off Celebes, as the modern tourist who comes
on deck one morning when his palatial liner, on
its way round the world, is making for Macas-
sar through the Spermondes, and who asks cheerfully, where are we now? One has to guess at the
track of the *Golden Hind* after Drake got her
out of the Bay of Gorontalo, which disappointed
him because he had entered it under the supposition that it was an east-and-west passage.

The most recent and the best edition of *The
World Encompassed*, which Mr. N. W. Penzer
edited for The Argonaut Press, boldly includes a
map devised to suggest Drake's course, after he
departed from Ternate, through an ocean which
is as remarkable with islands as is a dark clear
night with stars. The landfalls were named to
Drake's men by Malays; we may only guess at
the islands they sighted. A glance at current charts
of the east coast of Celebes and of the Banda and
Flores Seas, besprinkled as they are with soft but
outlandish names, is enough to warn us that if
today we were dependent only on the gentle
voice of a native pilot, with his tanjongs and
gunongs, we could do no better than Drake's men,
especially as friendly Malays occasionally name
an object to suit the taste of their questioners.

There is that excuse for Mr. Preacher Fletcher's
sketchy geography, but it does not altogether
show why fervour is fading from his narrative
by the time we are in the Moluccas. Those islands, and Java, did not appear to interest him
as much as plate ships. Yet let us be fair to him.
The precious *Cacafuego* was by good fortune
captured before the *Golden Hind* set a course into
the blue; after that happy occasion came the
crossing of the Pacific, a wide and anxious matter.
Then, when the Islands of the Kings were left,
and the meridian of the journey was past, doubtless the men of the *Golden Hind* had set their
minds on home; but they were met by adverse
winds in unknown seas perplexing with coral reefs
and strong tide rips. While they were wondering,
after their disappointment in the Bay of Gorontalo, when they would clear that everlasting coast
of Celebes, they ran aground; they must have
been thinking, by that time, much more of Dev-
onshire than of Spice Islands. Mr. Fletcher's attention to the novelties about him was dulled.
He was thinking of home, not of Java, and so
should we have been. Let us make that concession
to him; we are then free to ask why he is so vague
in his record of the Doughty affair, for Doughty
was executed before even the capture of the *Caca-*

57

fuego. Except the terrific buffeting of Drake's little fleet in the neighbourhood of Cape Horn—an episode in the voyage of which commentators have made hardly enough, for it was a miracle the adventurers survived—the execution of Doughty was till then the most remarkable event of the voyage; it must have echoed with heaven knows what intrigues of distant London and the court. Francis Drake was a just man, and it is hard to believe that he would have had Doughty put out of the way except on evidence which would stand the right tests. But what was it? Fletcher was present, yet what he offers are generalities which would be accepted today only by one who has made up his mind that a dog were better dead. Still, Preacher Fletcher's account of it is the most we shall get; for Drake's own record has gone the way of other personal testaments which we should value, if we could happen upon them, more than the discovery of fresh fields of oil. The parson's substitute, for all its quaintness, is certainly unappeasing in its bovine insensibility. Its bucolic heartiness over trivial affairs which, we may judge, Drake was barely aware of except that they indicated the healthy spirit of his men, and so dismissed, has not been without an unfortunate consequence.

popularly described, when it is wished to dismiss them as inappropriate and inclement, as "highbrow." The ways of such a mind appear to be unnatural; they will cut across the common routine, which is fairly safe for most of us, we have found, if we do not experiment with it too much; they are apart from the noticeable broad streams of human thought, for they usually come of reasoning which issues from premises quite other than those best suited to justify ordinary appetities. Those bluff sea-dogs would be in place in collier brigs, and at times would be tiresome enough there. No doubt in such ships, with such work, they could live their useful lives unnoticed in a rough and conducive environment. We may be quite sure they would be out of place if ever they attempted the navigation of ships, and the leadership of men, in uncharted seas where the problems were so abruptly challenging, so different from the commonplace of home waters, that the natural fearful doubts of crews had to be allayed with the continual successful determination of lurking shallows and unknown landfalls. Such a task required the maintenance of an art, and a faith in loneliness amid an alien world, possible only to men able to think and live apart. Useless, between Gilolo and Java, for mere sea-dogs to rely on bluff! That will not help a navigator in uncharted waters when a crew is sick and fearful. A master-mariner so situated must be as accurate in his estimates of time and place, and the moods of his men, as circumstances will allow to his science and experience. He may not trust to high spirits and the horseshoe over his cabin door. His design is to bring again to their home port his men and his ship with exactly what he set forth to add to human knowledge and wealth. Drake must have known, as Cook certainly knew, that it is the incompetent leader, or the ill-advised leader, who is almost sure to meet in his enterprise with those tragic happenings that bring a venture to ruin, and make what romantic commentators call "an epic story." Drake understood, as did Cook, that the chance of tragedy frustrating a venture may be lessened by prudence, good knowledge, and bold judgment. Such explorers do not set out to find an epic story, but to add to verified things and the welfare of their fellows. Drake was an imaginative man, but his essays with the unknown were under the control of a patient and calculating mind.

A careful reading of Fletcher's account of the first English voyage round the world reveals the sea-dog in command as one whose success with his

bold and original tactics awoke in simple souls
only a faith in his lucky audacity; he was, they
saw, like one of the old Greek heroes, a favorite
of the gods. It ought to be clear to us that he was
a wary leader, with his desires under strict discipline. He never ordered his men to a risk where
he judged the cost of failure would be more than
the expedition could afford to pay. He withdrew
from a project, or withheld an attack upon what
seemed rich and unsuspecting prey, if his estimate gave him too much to doubt. Drake's intention was to extend the influence of the English;
the right of the Pope to divide the outer seas and
continents between Spain and Portugal he ignored; those countries could only monopolize the
riches of America and the Orient if they could
keep out English seamen, and he did not think
they were able to do that. Their monopoly he
intended to challenge, whatever his own sovereign
might think; he was as astute as Elizabeth, but
whereas she temporized with the threatening
powers about her, retarding the crisis, for she was
not so sure as her seamen that the Spanish colossus was growing unstable, Drake, when he could
be sure of his blow, struck at it, and left the awkward consequence to the politicians. He was confident the English could safely defy august and

" . . . out of soundings"

ancient prohibitions, and could go where they
chose, when prepared as he and Hawkins and
Frobisher knew how to prepare ships and men.
To him the seas were free, and he could deal with
those who tried to take the wind out of his sails.
An English voyage to America then was unlaw-
ful, and Drake was a pirate and transgressor
whenever he held too far to the westward; but he
intended that English seamen should destroy the
fanciful bounds of Spanish dominion. Preacher
Fletcher would be unaware of this; he was not
told.

Drake contemplated an end that was out of
sight of his companions; his lucky audacity was
that only to surprised and admiring followers on
whom he had not wasted time beforehand with
an exposition of his reckoning. We may suppose
that cheerful Mr. Fletcher fell into the common
error of seeing an original and masterful character, keeping its own counsel safe from the cor-
ruption of debate, merely as a man whose virtues
were common to all, but by Drake were expressed
with greater courage and clarity. That is a view
which is flattering to us. Thus the sea-dog is one
of us, but a little better. The original character
is ordinary, after all, yet somewhat larger than
usual. It does not otherwise differ; and so we

resolve a forgivable fear and dislike of a difference in nature. When the hidden processes of personality manifest superiority with an unmistakable success, a success which would have been sheer luck had it come our way, then it can be disenchanted by attributing it to perseverance, pluck, and good fortune. What could Fletcher do, when he saw Drake in action? Nothing but the beginning of that legend of the jolly and rough sea-dog.

Drake was not only the most remarkable of Elizabeth's seamen, but his cabin, so to speak, was in a ship his men could not enter; their knowledge could not find it; he was already a leader of an Empire that had not come, and he seems to have guessed it. He did have, it must be admitted, to aid him in this, some gifted friends and colleagues. It must be remembered that England then was a poor country. The common idea of its opulence is wrong; but, as evidence that it had come of age and was outgrowing its confines, it was rich with an astonishing number of discerning and energetic politicians, merchants, soldiers, and sailors. They may not have been conscious of what was stirring them, but they meant to get out of a back room. In Mr. McFee's biography of Sir Martin Frobisher he doubts that scholars of a

peaceful temperament should attempt to write
history; and certainly that period of the English
in which came the Reformation, the overthrow
of Latin dominion, the poetry of Shakespeare,
and the beginning of the British Commonwealth,
suggests that it is not easy for anyone to write
history, for it is a curious fact that no scholar has
yet attempted to make a full and reasonable story
of those years in a way which would be of significance to us, though the attractions of the subject are notable, and invite a life-long devotion.
It surprises Mr. McFee that the Elizabethan
poets left it to Dutchmen and others to magnify
the deeds of English seamen. Tennyson, every
child knows—or it was common knowledge with
children before 1914—sang the glory of the
Light Brigade at Balaclava. Shakespeare, however, who knew of Drake's great voyage, and very
likely saw the *Golden Hind* at Deptford, and
who, if he did not hear the Armada's guns, at
least saw the heralding beacon fires and knew
their dread import, is silent on it all, or at most is
briefly allusive. What was the matter with him
and his fellow singers? Even though the wine at
the Mermaid Tavern were thin stuff, here were
matters which were inspiriting without wine.
But the world encompassed by an English ship,

the fears and gossip which grew out of news from the Continent of Spain's preparation of a vast armament, the beacon lights which at last signalled the danger offshore, and then the news that the Spanish fleet was scattered, left the English poets still seeking their themes in mediæval romance and classical lore. However, it is worth noting, meanwhile, that we are still waiting for an epic poem entitled Ypres. Troy has one, but not Ypres.

There is but scant material for a close biography of Frobisher. That leader of Tudor seamen was quick-tempered, loyal to his friends, bold to recklessness in action, and knew as much of his trade as would a man of energy and enterprise who was most of forty years in ships, exploring, slave-hunting, and fighting; he was the discoverer of Davis Strait, and the first Englishman to attempt to found a colony on the American continent. He was so tall and strong that once he grabbed an Eskimo paddling alongside the ship, and lifted him inboard, complete with canoe and weapons. That feat, as Mr. McFee explains, says something about the freeboard of a ship then daring the unknown Arctic. Nevertheless, though such incidents are delightful to youthful readers, they do not greatly help a biographer towards a portrait of a man, with a reasonable guess at his period for a background. His biographer, therefore, is compelled to use Frobisher as a tentative introduction to sixteenth-century Europe with its inherencies that later were to develop into American civilization. That theme is immense, but it is, for the most part, out of soundings. Those Tudor days, compared with the long stretch of human history, are only just off the current calendar; yet the motives of the actors developing that drama which is now materially manifest in the skyscrapers of New York, and playing their parts either deliberately, or under the ægis of Zeus, or moved by the fateful time-spirit which is much more mysterious than was the prompting of the gods to the people within and without the walls of Troy, are often as inscrutable as the spread of plasm in a coral reef. So, we remember, were the motives of the counsellors of Europe, as their memoirs show, whose knowledge and desires brought that continent to war and revolution in our own day. Mr. McFee wonders why the Tudor poets were dumb about their own romantic time; so do we. That is one of the problems which arise from his provocative and lively biography of an Elizabethan seaman. We see in that problem, to our surprise, another

of the wonders of Gloriana's reign, and it is
enough to check the most flamboyant of the historians of our own great war and our still more
remarkable peace. Who will expound it for us?
For the man who wrote *King Lear* is silent
about it; he ignores the sensational events which
must have caused nearly all the talk on Tudor
quaysides and in the taverns of London. Can there
be a complete and satisfactory answer? Clearly
we dare not say that Shakespeare was what is now
called, disdainfully, a "pacifist," and that therefore he was aware—he was aware of most of the
things which disturb us, which check us with
doubts—that as a historian he would be mean and
inadequate. Yet, even so, he might still have celebrated the triumphs of his great contemporaries?
Well, he did not.

We note, in passing, that even Mr. McFee,
when he mentions Gloriana, is not too circum-
spect with her regal splendour and her undoubted
genius; he thinks her parsimony was near to in-
sanity. It really does seem so. Had the crisis been
left to her, then the Spaniards might not have
seen an English warship in the Channel. We see,
too, that the biographer of so honest a man as
Frobisher will not leave us undisturbed with our
rosy supposition that it was pure patriotism which

took English ships to sea to meet Spain's Armada; he advises us that the hope of loot was also strong. The English ships had scant ammunition, they were badly provisioned, and their men were wanting their wages. They were anxious to meet those Spaniards; they were not in the least impressed by the size and the scrollwork of the enemy's galleons, nor by the Papal blessing upon them. They had learned, in their rough schooling, that they had more seaworthy ships, and were better seamen and better gunners, that they could get their vessels to go about while a portentous enemy was lumbering to leeward full of dignity and wounded men; Drake and the rest of them hoped to make the Spaniards pay. It may be possible, it is fair to suggest, that the lazy poets who frequented the Mermaid Tavern knew what Mr. McFee knows. Expanding commerce, the increase of a nation's estates, and the discovery of loose gold, are good; yet in some important ways they are not good enough. It is not easy to be lyrical over them. They are not easily translated into noble music. I do not suggest that this is why the Elizabethan poets were dumb when their age was so resounding with guns and fanfares, yet certainly they must have known Grenville better than Tennyson, though they have said less

71

about him. For our part, that would make an entertaining romance if a writer could come to the inner truth of it, that international trustification of the chemical industry, with Lord Melchett, audacious and wise, presiding in what is the modern equivalent of the admiral's cabin of the *Golden Hind*, that guarded room where meet privileged company-promoters and directors; yet perhaps the very suggestion that music should be made of it would set Athene's owl hooting.

The canny bird would hoot at it. But it is safe to dare the suggestion that Shakespeare did as well, in his own way, as the great sea-captains of Gloriana; and, incidentally, that a poet may now be singing, even unheard, because far in our own background, who will be remembered when all the chemicals of Lord Melchett's international trust are dissolved. There was more accomplished in Elizabeth's time than the shattering of the Spanish colossus, and the clearing and settling of New World sites for Mr. Ford's automobile factories and such. Today we can fly around the world, and count the journey in days, not years; and, even so, it is just beginning to dawn on us, with this new power to our hand controlled by levers described as fool-proof, that we do not know our whereabouts, precisely, but must discover it. The globe must again be encompassed; our explorers must be guided by stars Drake never saw in his heavens. An industrious New World, though equipped with machinery that could supply an automobile and an aeroplane to every villa, cannot help humanity in its new voyage of discovery to learn its whereabouts and a right course; that essential truth cannot be found with an output of standardized machinery which is even prodigious in its magnitude.

While now you are observing your ship approach Tanjong Priok, and are noting the violet heights beyond of central Java, an aeroplane may pass overhead, and a submarine may be in view. These may serve us as signs of a control, "foolproof," as the saying is, of our visible world, where once were truculent rajahs ashore, and head-hunters at sea. The aeroplane and the submarine suggest control of the good things for particular peoples; and it was to secure such a control, by the English, which was the compelling thought of Drake. Control? We know now, unluckily, that Western man's insatiable curiosity and inventiveness have at last added factors to discovery which have disturbed the foundations of the profitable order it was Drake's intention, and ours, to establish like granite. For today, among the islands which Drake's men looked upon with awe and surprise, and only three and a half centuries ago, wireless telephony, the cinematograph and Moscow are making insidious differences and antipathies; they are rousing the once docile populations of those large cities built in the East to the needs of a Western culture, densely populated by Chinamen and others to whom that culture is alien, and even hateful, and can never be in harmony. The world discovered—no, only rediscovered—by Tudor navigators, has changed more since their recent day than it had in the thousand years before Henry the Navigator began to make old things new again in the seas where the explorations of the Egyptians and the Phœnicians were forgotten. It will have to be discovered and mapped anew, by us. Yet to what end? That end, we are beginning to guess, is far beyond the range of the interests which dispatched Drake's fleet from Plymouth to encompass the earth. Its exploration will, we must admit, demand of us precisely those virtues by which Drake found his way round the globe against the opposition of the King of Spain and the Pope's prohibition, to the Islands of the Kings; qualities of character that made him noteworthy but misunderstood in years of

turies ago. Venturers from the Mediterranean went through the Pillars two thousand years before Henry's day, but what they had found was lost. How far they ventured it is impossible to say, but certainly they went far. It is safe to assume there were men before the dawn of history who had a fund of lore and skill beside which the culture of most of the inhabitants of our modern cities would seem helpless and savage. When the Saxons were so behaving in England that historians cannot say much about them, except that they were destructive, two centuries before Alfred began to civilize them, the Javanese were voyaging to Madagascar, Zanzibar, and China. Archæologists are speculating over the resemblance of rites of the Solomon Islanders to those known in ancient Egypt. It has been wondered why craft on some rivers of the Far East resemble so closely those which anciently navigated the Mediterranean. A more remarkable attribute of man than his eager curiosity which compels him to discover is the tenacity with which he sticks to old things, and especially to old opinions. The knowledge that something may be done in another and a better way satisfies him; he does not want to attempt that way; and at length he forgets the fact. A new and significant discovery will stir his interest, yet the next odd fact, perhaps of less significance, will distract his attention, and so the first discovery sinks out of sight of human knowledge, maybe for half a millennium. Man really is never in a hurry, in spite of the illusion of the well-advertised aerodromes which mark the route from London to Baghdad.

We have to note in Fletcher's narrative his increasing dislike for the coast of Celebes, which is as attractive a mountainous shore as the seas can offer. The *Golden Hind* tried to work round the north of that island, and failed. She attempted passage to the south, and was three days retreating from the deep Gulf of Gorontalo, which was imagined to be a thoroughfare; it was there that the Spaniards and the Portuguese hoped that Drake would get lost. Drake worked his ship farther south, against head winds, and presently ran her upon a bank of live coral. English mariners then were not used to live coral. The *Golden Hind* was held to the edge of the bank by the wind, but at length she heeled towards deep water, and, "freed her keele and made us glad men. Of all the dangers that in our whole voyage we met with, this was the greatest; but it was not the last, as may appear by what ensueth. Neither could we indeed for a long season free ourselves from the continual care and fear of them; nor could we ever come to any convenient anchoring, but were continually for the most part tost among the many Islands and shoales (which lye in infinite number round about the South part of Celebes) till the eight day of the following month."

The ship took a month to clear that coast, and Fletcher, reflecting, we may suppose, the mood of the majority of his companions, grew a little desperate at the enduring uncanny picture of those tumbled forested crags in a torrid glare to starboard; that strange coast had put a spell upon them. The novelty of Celebes did not attract him. His curiosity in wonders was glutted; he did not want to know what mysteries were hidden by those green heights. He says:

"Jan. 12, being not able to beare our sayles, by reason of the tempest, we let fall our anchors upon a shoale in 3deg. 30min. Jan. 14, we were gotten a little further South, where, at an Island in 4deg. 6min., we againe cast anchor, and spent a day in watering and wooding. After this wee met with foule weather, Westerly winds, and dangerous shoales for many dayes together; insomuch that we were utterly weary of this coast

78

of Sillebis, and thought best to bear with Timor."
That, in general, is what the coast of Celebes is
like today. A seaman must repel its enticement,
and be very prudent, when in sight of its forests.
A few steamers call regularly at certain points
of it, but its primitive aspect, its appearance of
having been just like that since time began, has
not altered since the *Golden Hind* was beating
about there, in spite of our aeroplanes. Its interior is still largely unexplored.

It was in November, 1579, that Drake was
at Ternate. He was most kindly received by the
Sultan and his people. Fletcher grows lyrical over
the benefits of that delightful little island kingdom, where the *Golden Hind* found some of the
happiest days of her long travail. What is progress? In those very waters, in 1844, the *Sama-
rang*, a British warship, in the command of an
experienced navigator, and also on a voyage of
exploration, destroyed some native craft and
many of the people, including women and children, in what was but a silly panic that arose out
of ignorance. Nothing had been gained in three
hundred years; something had been lost; good
will was shot away. It is easier to use a gun than
to show courage. When Drake was anchored off
Ternate he must often have seen the immense

spectacle of sunrise over the mountains of Gilolo, or Halmaheira, the main island across the strait, and watched at sunset the colours which then make its peaks unearthly. Drake must have thought it an enchanted region, of incredible richness, a Paradise to which he was but opening the door. In his day the Spice Islands were but a romantic name, a call to adventurers; and here he was, at long last. So slowly does man come to knowledge, and so easily does he forget, that Gilolo is still exactly as he saw it. Even Wallace did not venture into its interior, which is hardly better known than when Drake viewed its mountains from Ternate.

If one turns to the current *Directions for Pilots*, the volume for the Eastern Archipelago, printed for the Hydrographic Office of the Admiralty, it is possible to read such an entry as this, concerning the Moluccas: "Ceram Island has not been hitherto thoroughly explored, for the interior consists, especially in the west, of mountainous country, with dense forests and peopled by savages, who are by no means well disposed to Europeans." Or this: "Taliabu (of the Sula Islands), the westernmost and largest, is very little known." There are many others, for which the directions to mariners are just as explicit and admonishing. Even the world we have "encompassed" is not quite well known to us yet; we have not made much of it, so far, even on its material side since Henry the Navigator began to show the way, and the industrial revolution followed soon with its cheap cotton, its coal and iron, and latterly with its destroyers, aeroplanes, submarines, the cinematograph and Karl Marx. Before even our cheap cotton has got to Taliabu we must begin the encompassing of this so newly discovered world with an idea or two which may serve to hold it securely together. The world has been explored, it may be, too fast and too casually. Pioneers did not quite know where they were going, nor exactly what they wanted to do with a place when they had found it. And in this new exploration, in the hope of a light which will help us to make the best of a world of which at present we know but the superficies not too well, let the instance of Preacher Fletcher be a warning. We may hitherto have attached too much importance to bluff sea-dogs.

❡ A Lost Wood

A critic of letters was discussing the French Romantics, and he dismissed, with but an impatient glance at it, a suggestion by one of us that Rousseau was a harbinger of the Revolution. Literature, so the critic said, could do less to cause a general uproar than dear bread. Books, one gathered from the critic, and he knew more of them than did we who listened, were quite unrelated to the emotions of the multitude, which discharged in thunder and lightning provoked no more by poetry than by daisy-chains.

The critic may have been right. I expect the change in us wrought by poetry is so slow in the showing that when the transmutation is complete we know of no change. We cannot see what has happened to us. The poet, having done in his brief life his best, may get what comfort he can out of that. We are certainly obstinate in our old ways, conservative with flint arrowheads or any other familiar notion, and unmoved by revolutions which come about in imperceptible degrees. And could Sinai itself impose its revelation on a climber who was no Moses? All most of us would discern at the summit of Sinai would be

the uncomfortable draught sweeping the barren
rocks.

It is probable, we are forced to confess, that
a few years of petrol have made a greater difference in the world of men than all the poets since
Homer. To judge by the reformed highways and
byways of England, and the talk of our neighbours, petrol has moved us more than all our converse with great literature. Petrol is more popular
than religion, and whirls to delight a vast multitude of people who would remain as unaffected
by Bach as a congregation of penguins. If the test
were made, perhaps a little argument directed
towards a choice of the right sort of motor-
car might more easily raise a group of people to
eloquence than an insult to the Trinity. Petrol is
even dissolving the face of the English landscape.
We are exchanging our woodlands for tarmac,
and although tarmac is known to be kind to rub-
ber tyres, yet its tolerance is hardly sufficient to
compensate for the loss of swathes of orchards,
meadows, and ancient buildings. One does not
complain about this, for it would be just as foolish to complain of the untimeliness of a phase
of the moon.

Yet regret and disquietude, despite the improvements we are making in our condition, re-

main with us, for we cannot forget our poets and what once inspired them to sing. Once there was a scrap of Surrey, which I had grown to accept as casually as one does those things whose importance is known when they are gone. I think it was only common English countryside. There was nothing in it that a building contractor should desire it. Nobody with an eye to the future saw anything there. Its gravel soil was not worth an advertisement. But it had a desultory lane, with walnut, lime, and beech trees, and on a morning in late summer you were not likely to meet anything in it but a farm waggon laden with dried peppermint; mint and lavender were cultivated locally, and our only factories had stills for the extraction of essences from herbs. The smell in the wake of that waggon on a hot day gave a surprising suggestion of the virtue of Surrey earth.

I could not say the war began to change it, but it seems so. I do know that one part of the land, and corn grew there, through which the lane meandered, became very swiftly an aerodrome; and the aerodrome has not yet convinced me that it is better to see flying-machines at their graceful evolutions than a field of wheat with a little wind and much sun on it. Alas! We were

too busy then to consider in calmness the nature
of the change we were bringing about. I remember that, in the years of long ago, before we were
educated even so far as the signs of Zeppelins by
night, we had neighbouring ponds fed by springs
in the chalk. At the bottom of one deep trans-
parent pool you could see a spring uprising;
shadows coiled in the beryl. That was where,
within twelve miles of Charing Cross, we watched
a pair of kingfishers feeding their six youngsters;
the babies sat in a row on an osier twig, which
was oblique with their weight. The darting blue
and chestnut of those neighbours of ours greatly
distinguished us. One lucky young friend of mine
saw in the same secluded grove, and as late as
the days of the air-raids, a golden oriole. He
still remembers it. To hear him you might suppose that one day on his way home from school,
where he had been learning of the brave things
that were, he had surprised a dryad, who slipped
into the bushes, but not before he could name her.
Does Apollo live? So much was possible to him,
that day.

Does he live? Well, not there; not now. Petrol
has acted like magic on the place. Miraculous
stuff, petrol! But the kingfishers do not like it.
Nor does the lane wander any more. It has been

disciplined, and we know how good is discipline. The lane is broad, it is direct. It has no dust, and has lost its smell of herbs. The old walnut trees do not lean over broken pales there. There are no trees. The lane has become a straight road with a surface like polished ebony. It is, in fact, a high-way for motor-cars. It becomes dangerous, every Sunday morning, with an endless flying procession of engines on their way to the coast; the chain reverses towards evening. We do not hear the corncrake any more, when coolness and silence fall at eventide; we hear klaxons. We have no peppermint fields; we have filling stations. Our springs and ponds, owing to an increase in the value of gravel sites, have lapsed into areas of mud which cannot determine to dry completely, and are desolate with discarded tins. As for the golden oriole, you might as well look for a seraph. Petrol has achieved all that. We do not say a word against it, but merely point to the fact. It would be just as useful to interrupt, as a protest, the line of cars flying to the coast on a Sunday, in a moment of desperation and anger. There the cars are; they move faster than peppermint waggons, and modern youth often steers them in a fashion that mocks mortality.

It is easy to understand the popularity of petrol.

As a stimulant, it is taking the place of beer and whiskey. Rousseau may not have helped to cause a revolution, but there is no doubt about the common emotion which petrol evokes. Petrol is taken, not in the hope that it will transport us to any better place, but merely that it will remove us swiftly from where we are. It is the latest anodyne in these years of discontent and irresolution. It would be ridiculous to expect us to know what we ought to do, for we do not always know what we want to do. Petrol settles the difficulty. We get into a car, and start the explosions within its powerful engine; then we are compelled to do something. We join an endless line of headlong vehicles; and to continue to be irresolute would be perilous. Last summer I trudged over a road, once a by-path in the West of England which a tramp could have for himself for most of a long day. I hoped there to meet a ghost or two from the past, because they used to know that road very well, and they might turn up, if the news got to them that I was there again. But I did not meet them. I met instead a procession of astonishing charabancs, some from Manchester, others from Birmingham, and one from as far as Glasgow. There was no room for a pedestrian but in the drains by the roadside, where he had to stride for safety through soiled nettles and briars. The local inns were no longer places of refreshment and gossip. About one of those inns, and I had had my mind set on it for an hour, a dozen huge social cars were parked. The road was bright with pools of black grease. The orchard of the inn was sad, through traffic for which orchards are not grown. And no room could be had at the bar, nor elsewhere within, for an idle traveller who had time to waste; other travellers were there, continually arriving and departing. They had no time to waste. Yet these travellers of the new kind appeared to be satisfied merely with travelling. They knew not why they were there; they had paid their fares. They stood about, waiting for the signal that they were to be whirled on again, with their backs to a land which is as good as most in Europe. They did not look at it. It did not exist in its reality for them; it was only on their route. They were satisfied with the knowledge that they were there; they could prove it with picture-postcards, which could be bought at the inn counter.

Very early one morning, when on a voyage from the East, I was startled from sleep by a seaman. He had switched on my light. It was summer, but he stood there chilling the cabin with his wet overcoat. What was wrong?

"Nothing, sir; the chief officer wants you on the bridge."

I went up hurriedly, in pyjamas and oilskins. Day had not come, but it was not night; night was lifted slightly in the east on a wedge of rose, though the wind was still bleak out of darkness. We were somewhere near the Berlengas. What was this? My friend the chief officer pointed astern without a word. We were passing a ghost ship, under all canvas. The barque was so close that I could see the length of her deck. She was silent, and more pale than the twilight. She was tall, and tinctured faintly with rose. Had we steamed back into another age? Was the past so near? I could see two men on her poop, but they were not looking at us. Only my friend, and the bridge of our liner, were material. My friend spoke. "I thought you would like to see her; it may be the last time. Isn't she a beauty?"

Even with my eye still on the receding barque I felt that sailor's behaviour was more curious than what he had wakened me to watch. His jacket, I had noticed, bore a row and a half of decorations won in war; he was a hard and busy officer; he infested that great liner as a stern challenge whose whereabouts was uncertain until he strode round a corner, and then he never stopped unless there was something which must be said. This unexpected tenderness of his for what was hardly more than a gracious apparition in a delusive hour surprised me; yet he had been so sure, and without reason, that I, too, would have the eye to see the spectre, that he had summoned me from bed into the hour when there is no courage. We stood talking up aloft till the sun came and saw us.

So though I dare not deny the critic who mocked the power of poetry to work upon us to as good a purpose as starvation, yet perhaps he was too trifling with the spell of what is imponderable. Our mutability, like the wind which bloweth where it listeth, is subject to sorceries having the necessity of the very laws which send zephyrs or hurricanes out of the immane. How often has a fond memory or sentiment, so doubtfully valid in garish daylight that we would not show it to a friend, decided us in an enterprise? And we were right. For that reason, the older we get the more we doubt the obvious clue to any story; we have found too often that what was unrevealed at the time was more potent than anything we heard when the knowing people were

explaining it. But for a barque appearing near
our liner one morning, I should have thought
my friend the chief officer was no more open to
zephyrs and faint hints than the steel under us.
That steel was obvious and compelling, and he
was part of it. And after that voyage he sent a
letter to me, disclosing a burden which not for a
moment did I suspect a modern liner to carry.
He was glad, he explained, to get out of London
again. He called his steamer's bridge, which to
me seemed to govern affairs large and complex
enough to require a borough council for their
management, his sanctuary. He showed a repul-
sion from our city which was as spontaneous and
unreasonable as would be a mahatma's from a
riot. He said his bridge, in the morning watch,
was the only place where he could meet himself.
He warned me that in London I should never
meet myself. London frightened him. London
was on no course. London was adrift. Its size
and unrest were so like delirium that he ran from
it. "Those new buildings you've got, they're
Egyptian I tell you, they're horrible. Something
has gone wrong with you if you like them. You'd
better look out. They squat on the mind, ugly
square masses, like tombs. I don't want to be
under them, as though I had no name, drifting

at the bottom of them with the drainage of life which doesn't know where it is going. It doesn't, does it?" He said he found himself again only when watching his ship's head grow bright in the dawn, and nothing around but the empty sea and the sun. Then he knew his name belonged to him, and what he was doing, and why he was doing it, to some extent.

Perhaps rebellion comes as much as anything from the sense that, as mere items in the paraphernalia of the State, we are losing our identity. A slave may have a soul, and possess it in patience, but not an automaton. Made homogenous by machinery, we have but one name now; we are the nation. And when our governing machines, multiplying and expanding, claiming greater space for their wheels, flatten and unify still more the ancient, varied, and familiar things which we did not know were good till they had gone, we feel as though our identity will soon be traceless. We become a little fearful and desperate. It is as though a chilling air were felt from unseen ice gradually advancing, warning of another glacial age, to put our names and works with the Neanderthalers. We rebel from the suggestion that we must go under the cold mass of a mindless necessity.

92

It was April; and that was a disturbing letter
to receive when the primroses were due. I had
no chance to reassure myself of my name by
watching a ship's head grow bright in a broad
dawn; Egypt for me, and the necessary rod! All
I could do was to rebel for a day. I would decline to make a single brick. I began to walk away
from the arid masses of London's honeycombed
limestone, monuments of servitude, though was
careful to begin my escape at the ten-mile radius.
I remembered that it was some years since I had
walked in that direction, for the paths I used to
know appeared to have been mislaid. Escape was
not so easy from new, wide, straight, and as-
phalted thoroughfares dangerous with swift
engines. Aeroplanes were chanting overhead, but
no larks. A raw inflammation of villas was spread-
ing through a valley, which was green when last
I saw it. Then my companion, he who once met
a golden oriole, remembered a little wood in a
hollow, aside from the traffic. That, he told me,
would certainly be there. Nobody would have
interfered with that. He found the lane to it,
after some bewilderment with his bearings, which
had shifted somewhat. There was no doubt that
this was the lane, he declared at last, but du-
biously. It was? Then we must suffer it, erupted

and raw. Its hedges, bearing the first leaves of the year, were displaced, and their roots were higher than their boughs. In some lengths of the lane granite kerbs had replaced the hedges, and an iron sink-hole or two improved the ditches. A new path, a motor-lorry careened midway in its deep mud, went directly into the wood. On the verge of the wood the hazels had been crushed and splintered, and their golden tassels hung disconsolate, as though we were on the track of a recent and lusty mastodon.

Improvement had come. In the heart of the wood oaks were being felled, and by the torn roots of one was a dead hedgehog, which had been turned out of its hybernaculum into the frigid blast of reform. Unseen towards the heart of the wood a saw was at work, and its voice was like the incessant growling of a carnivore which had got its teeth into a body and would never let go. This Easter, by all the signs, was the last the wood would see. The bluebells had been coming, expecting no evil, and had they been allowed the grace of a few more weeks they would have put the depth of the sky between the trees; but carts and engines had crushed them, and had even exposed their white bulbs, as though the marrow of the wood were exposed.

I do not say the Easter message of that wood was especially deplorable. I knew it was possible and even right to see those granite kerbs and the cleared foundations as an urgent message of life and growth. The children of men would play in new gardens there, in another Easter. Still, somehow that direct and unquestioning attack by our machines, especially on the fragile windflowers, was more dismaying than inclement weather. A mastodon might really have been there, with no mind but in its tusks, irresistible and forthright. "I thought you would like to see her; it may be the last time. Isn't she a beauty?" It may be that the sense of beauty has no survival value, to use a term of our biological appraisers; nevertheless, it does survive, so we may suppose there is something as primordial in it as in acquisitiveness. When we see the defacement of beauty we continue to feel as though light were put out in ignorance. And what we want, as certainly as new villas, is more light. Is there a light to check us when steering our wheels over the windflowers, the Pasque blossoms, and are replacing them with stones?

There were Greek pagans long ago, and some of their work clearly had a value by which, though not useful, it has survived; and the idle fancy was theirs that the windflower was stained with the blood of Adonis, slain by a boar, and that its pallor was from the tears of Aphrodite, who sorrowed over the beautiful youth. Even our own pagans, before Augustine gave their thoughts another direction, felt bound to conclude that the windflower was painted by the elves. Who else could have veined so delicately that fabric? Who else would have inspired daintiness with that modesty in the half-light of the woods?

Behind me I heard the motor-lorry heaving itself out of the mire it had made. It backed and crashed like a hippopotamus into another tracery of mist and emerald, and Adonis died again. I buttoned up my coat against the northerly blast. Let Adonis die. We cannot help him. The tears of Aphrodite are of no avail against the tusks of boars. Only the bolts of Zeus could prevail against the progress of our engines; and Olympus, we have been most credibly informed for many Easters past, is "to let"; and if we must believe the reports of our busy agents of estates, then it is about the only place that is to let.

Yet one of the things I clearly remember of the war was a bluebell. It was in Thiépval wood. Men who have reason to keep in mind the valley of the Ancre will smile at that. Thiépval had

"... the windflower ... its pallor was
from the tears of Aphrodite"

come to its end. Our engines had been there, had
gone over it, and were loudly progressing elsewhere on the eastern hills. It was April, but there
was no wood, no village, and no old château,
though a little down the slope towards St. Pierre
Divion was a tank on its side; one of the auto-
mata, too, had died. Life had gone; nothing was
there but mud, bones, rags, helmets, broken rifles,
and skulls. Thiépval was Golgotha. We were
turning from it, but were stopped by a fleck of
colour in the drab wreckage; life had already
returned to Thiépval? It was a wild hyacinth.
One bluebell to all April! What, still there and
unafraid?

One may dare to hope that the marrow of
earth has a more stubborn vitality than our dismay
allowed; it may survive our engines? It survived
the glaciers. After all, there may be in the frail
windflower a virtue that will outlast the lorries.
We have been surprised, before this, by the shy
patience of what may have been lovely and of
good report, yet otherwise was inexcusable. The
slight but haughty gesture of my sailor friend,
one dawn, saluting from the bridge of his ship
the beauty of the world, no more valuable though
it was than the pagan thought which celebrated
Adonis in the petals of the windflower, may have

been a sign that nothing could deflect a barque
he knew from her right course. And how else
could he prove his faith? He summoned me as
a witness, he was so sure of fellowship. Yet there
are no mathematics to support him.

The Wreck

We turned our heads as the door creaked and opened, admitting another man to the tavern, and giving a brief peep of ships in a morning harbour. This stranger in the village curtly acknowledged our company, which appeared to know him.

"Floated her yet?" he was asked, gently, as he stood at the bar. The question caused some faint ribald laughter. The stranger did not smile, nor look at us. He answered at leisure. "Expect us always to save ships you farmers chuck about like haycocks?" he enquired, genially.

He was a meagre fellow, with the lean face of a jockey who still had the saturnine visage for a hard race, but was past the age for riding. He did not look like a seaman; but then a seaman seldom does, unless other seamen doubt him. He might have been a pedlar, yet his demeanour was without the proper suavity. He could have been a tout, perhaps a bookmaker's, and that was why he was confident; he had found it easy to gain a fair share of the profits which come of quick traffic with human foolishness. His business might have been anything in which wit had a chance to devise good luck out of the slowness of respectable citizens. More likely he was a long-shoreman. His clothes were neutral in the dinginess and tobacco mist of that inn of a west-country harbour.

The stranger drank his beer, while meditating reproachfully a shabby gull in a glass case. He was asked how long he reckoned the job would take. He merely shifted his cap in ironic thoughtfulness. His cloth cap was an old and subdued subject, but it took on life as soon as he briskly pushed it back while considering a question, and then gave it a jaunty pull over his eyes. He looked up from under its peak in pained wonder at your innocence.

That cap had a chief part in his conversation. He was a Cockney as soon as he spoke. His comments on life and affairs were summary and sardonic, but his countenance was rigid. Only his thin lips and his cap moved. His eyes expressed fortitude for folly and misfortune but no surprise. There was some talk of the ships in harbour; several steps led down from the tavern entrance to the sanded floor, so we could see the ships outside riding curiously high in an upper light. Our eyes were drawn to the topmasts in the bright morning above the lower curtains of the windows. The stranger did not look that way.

He had his back turned to the light. He knew ships, as tokens of a hard life, and so, I suppose, he turned his back on them. Ships never came his way, he explained, except when they were no good.

His cap, in its artful inconsequence, helped him then with his allusions to large maritime enterprises, which he indicated briefly in grotesque outlines. They were burlesque adventures on the deep; the ironic fancies of a humorist who took that way of mocking the pretences of the sailors in that saloon bar. The sailors laughed, and did not deny him. His banter was too dry and townish. His seascapes were parodies of heroic weather, caricatures of the mighty deep, and raised a startled interest in an enormity at which one laughed. He knocked at the porch of Davy Jones in an absent-minded way. He entertained us with hints of desolate ships that had no rudders—one had no bottom—ships of a buoyancy which gave men hanging to them about five minutes more. Ships of malignant caprice, in league with cunning seas, prolonging the misery of crews who knew they were fools to be there. He assumed an attitude of patient resignation. The work of this little grey man was, in fact, salvage. He was there then on just such a job.

He was amusing, but that did not make it easy to see him directing the release of a ship, a sad victim, from the elemental powers which held her. I stood with him in the bow window of the tavern. The tide was flowing. We could see most of the broad water of the harbour. The sun was high. "There she is," he said. "That's mine."

That was his ship. His index finger was casually indifferent to her qualities. It was deprecative. I murmured warm approval of her usefulness. Tugs are indispensable vessels. She was a large tug. We talked of the handiness of tugs, and their remarkable power. The little skipper of the one in the harbour looked at his tug in friendly annoyance. "I shall be going out early this afternoon," he said. "Got nothing else to do? Come and see it."

He did not mean his ship. He meant this wrecked steamer which had caused furtive but jeering comment. That relic of tragedy was not to be seen from the village. The headland screened her. But she interested the village more than the news from London, and she would have been of more interest still had we known why she steered into such a corner on a clear night. Moved by the scandalous gossip, I thought I would like to see this Spaniard. That was why,

and for no better reason, I was aboard the tug
Hawk, listening to a Cockney on her bridge,
whose conversation had no more respect for romance or reality than is usual with a whimsical
man who has lived long enough to greet another
frustration with but a grimace.

His ship herself was a little whimsical. The
gear and lumber on her deck were adventitious
to seafaring, but by a cautious survey of it one
could climb and lower oneself the length of the
Hawk, and with few abrasions, for her length
was not great. One could reach the other end of
her in time and with care, and there was plenty
of time. The harbour was still, and the skipper's
allusive converse, while we waited, gave his ship
the unconvincing aspect of his cloth cap, which
was so much a part of his dry speech. I could
not be sure we were going anywhere to do anything. That did not matter. It was a shining and
spacious harbour, and the day was warm. An hour
of waiting in the midst of that historic water,
where the subdued muttering from mallets in the
shipyards, and the song of the tide, the sounds of
the life of our day, were only like slumberous
echoes from past centuries, made me feel that our
tug had no more to do with the next job than is

usual with the show of things when it happens to be pleasant in leisured and sunny retrospection.

Presently, however, I found I was forgotten. The past was mine, if I found it so pleasant. As for the skipper, he was addressing in a harsh foreign voice a group of men idling for'ard. He had suddenly lost his humour. We were, in fact, under way, and our quick passage from the still harbour to the ground-swell of the bay suggested how brief may be the transit, at times, from the bright and peaceful look of the day to the truth about it. The waters were moving largely. There was now no difficulty about getting to the other end of the *Hawk*; a careless passenger might be precipitated thither, in one movement.

We rounded the buoy which marks the beginning of the fairway to shelter, though we were not running for shelter, but otherwise. I was then at the first step of a journey from the stern companion-hatch to the wheel-house, when the tug, in my view of it, stood upright on her propeller. At least, it was necessary to wait a moment. Then there seemed to come an opportunity for a short run to a better handhold, but my intention was detected, and ten pounds of beef suspended in the rigging caught me with its bone-end. The movements of this ship were novel. Yet, though the fun of a lunatic does not win laughter, it must be respected. The ways of our tug with the seas were without order and precedent. She gave a hint of a lurch to port, and this passenger took it in time, only to learn that the hint was but an error which she corrected immediately, for she really wanted to roll to starboard. That became impossible, for the waters rose swiftly under her counter, and her funnel leaned over to look at the bow-wash, and so did her men. A little Atlantic voyage in a salvage steamer, with no stiffening but her pumps and dynamite, when a traveller begins to regret the steady home he has just left, offers him but one chance of peace; the giant powder may decide to get out of it.

In the northwest, over the waters of the bay which opens to all the Western ocean, we could see a low buff cloud, which was really an island. The gyrations of the *Hawk* made this land mark inconstant. We were lifted up, quivering in the wind, to see it far away, and then swashed into a cold hollow with a near view of a glassy wall falling past us. Down those fainting shadowy declivities we went, and then up again for another short glance round a distant horizon.

I sought the little man on the bridge. His cap was pulled down over his eyes, which had lost

their irony. He shook away the salt drops that
had struck his face. "We shall be out all night,"
he said.

All night! Then the only consolation in sight
was the slender stalk of the harbour light, and
that was diminishing astern. A strange coast was
growing larger over the port bow, high and re-
pellent, for the sun was descending behind it,
and I thought it remarkable that the huge boulders projecting from the steep black silhouette of
the promontory did not overbalance and fall, in
that wind and exposure. We were making for
that cape. The spray mounted noisy and spar-
kling at our bows, and fell over us. The day was
going, but the drenching helped the level evening
rays to make our ship lustrous, though bleak. We
approached the land, and the headland afforded
us some shelter, because now it stood over us almost to the zenith. We anchored; and we rolled.

The sun foundered in a bare waste, and the sea
fowl complained on the high dim shelves over
us. The world grew vague, though it was pouring
heavily past, and presently the moon, a full globe,
came to sit on the black jags above. That was
all there was to see, so I went below to sleep on a
hollow bench in which the dynamite was stowed.
The tug leapt and reared all night. To sleep, to

dream on uneasy dynamite, has its consequences, and at length it appeared to be better to go on deck and wait for morning. There I found the skipper, pacing his bridge in a great coat. "Don't want two wrecks here," he explained. "Must watch my cables."

His cables complained at their task. The moon had gone. A flurry of sparks, all I knew of the skipper's face, flew from his pipe. I heard him tap his pipe. An unseen comber, of greater weight, thundered on the invisible shore. The little man was but a shadow without shape on the rail of the weather-dodger. The shadow rose and came close to me. "I wish I knew," it grumbled. Our ship mounted with a panic of cables, and subsided again.

There was nothing for me to do but wait for the next word. A question of the tide in his mind —a possibility of approaching that wrecked steamer we had not sighted yet? Or the cables? The skipper was evidently considering again whatever doubt he had, because he was silent for a spell. "Well, there it is," he added. "There's no telling. Not," he remarked, "but what I sometimes think—but what's the good; you can think anything you like on a night like this. . . . D'ye hear that bird up there? Happy voice he's got, hasn't he?"

It was a call which accorded with the sounds of waters at night. Such cries are never answered. And what had a seamew to do with salvage work?

"I don't mind keeping a watch like this," the skipper mumbled, "because it gives me some time to myself. You can take your bearings on the quiet, if you can manage to pick 'em up. Think it over a bit. There's nothing else to do." He paused. "There's been heavy weather outside, to send this swell. Whoa, you brute! Sometimes— watch it, there's another coming!—sometimes I wonder whether it wouldn't be better to let the wreckage go. What's the bottom of the sea for? Let it all go. But you can't do it. Can't do it. You've got to let her have daylight while the pumps work. Eh? What do you think? That's right, isn't it? Keep her afloat, if it's no more good than whistling for a dead dog. Hold on to it. That's what I say. What do you say, mister?"

I held on when she listed, but said nothing. That sea bird called again. "Nice cheerful song- ster, that," said the skipper. He remained reflect- ing for a minute or two. Then he explained. "You see, what I always wanted was to give my boy a good start—don't begin at the bottom unless

" . . . *the triumphant waters shouted over her*"

you're there, that's sense, isn't it? Give him a
good start. He was quicker with a crayon than his
father with a blasting charge. He was a dab at
pictures, though I don't know how he picked it
up. But here we are. That boy talks now like that
bird up there; same sort of noise. But what would
you expect? He was never the same after he got
that bit of shrapnel in his head. What's the hope
that he ever will be? If I could only see the gist
of it . . ." He paused, idled over to a speaking-
tube, listened, and then bellowed to the bottom
of the tug.

"All right?" he cried. "Right. We're going to
move."

Day was coming. Night was leaving the dark
headland behind. The surges could be seen moving under its walls. We rounded that promontory,
and met the full strength of the west again. The
first of the dawn showed the leaning masts, for
they were white, of the wrecked steamer, the ship
which somehow had mistaken the sea lamps one
night, and had tried to cut off three miles of slate
and schist. In that wan light, in that welter of
jags and cataracts, with her deck at a woeful an-
gle, she affected a surprised witness as though she
were human and luckless. I turned to our skip-

113

per, and saw his profile clearly for the first time that morning. It was grey, stern, and worn.

What did I think? But I had not answered him. I was still trying to pick up the bearings. The skipper was unaware that I had looked at him intently. He stood up, and struck the rail with his hand. "Look at that!" he cried. "What's she doing there? That's a nice place for a visit."

I did not enjoy the look of it. Those cliffs, towards which the waters seemed to be flinging us, grew lighter. Their threat was serious. Less than that would have been enough. The wreck became plain under a descent of contorted strata, from which ribs and bosses protruded like the black bones of a dead earth. The master himself took the wheel, for our tug had begun to prance where the noises of the exploding waters was a daunting confusion. "We'll see if we can work in between the wreck and the shore," shouted the skipper. "What do you think?"

But in that, at least, he did not echo my mind, because not far from the *Hawk* I saw rocks threaten us with their bare teeth through the surf. Yet we closed the wreck. We rounded her stern and got under her lee. The seas were rocking her hull. They vaulted over her beam. We could hear her body groaning. The triumphant waters shouted over her, and occupied her with every breaker, then left her for a minute, with her deck a deep clear amythestine bath, through which her white paint glimmered till the instant when another wall of water from the ocean burst over all but her upper works.

"Here we are," said the skipper, alert and purposeful. "It's all right. We don't bump. We can start work."

❦Beauty and the Beast

A night or two ago I was persuaded to a first experience of The Talkies. It was explained to me that life is incomplete for one who has failed to watch a photographic story accompanied by appropriate words from a talking machine. Wonderful invention! It was a measure of our advance to higher and richer perceptions!

I confess I was reluctant to go. I do not remember that twenty years ago we were at all excited by the "talkies"; they were not wonderful then, but common to the week, and it was usual to attend them, for entertainment. Not so long since, when our Victorian souls desired light refreshment, we inclined to this or that music-hall, and we went to hear Marie Lloyd or Yvette Guilbert talk to us. Good talk it was, too.

Though not good enough for today, so we are told. We are assured it would not be good enough today. We have changed. There was a time, too, when we enjoyed witnessing a favourite conductor evoke from his instrumentalists Beethoven in a symphony; and then, in a dream, we could see that the timbalist, a vague presiding figure high above the rest of the orchestra, was Zeus himself, leisurely beating a measure for the spheres.

That respectful silence of the witnesses at the end of it, that brief pause when only the echoes of the music were sounding in one's mind, that was something, too; for we do not applaud on the instant what is noble as though it were a trick by a conjuror. We do not applaud because there is no surprise; there is but wonder. Our faith has always been that man, at rare intervals, may rise to such a height, and when he does so we are not surprised, but silenced.

Yet you cannot, by "wireless," see Zeus above measuring his thunder and flashes to the music. The radio set, that static little box of tricks we substitute for a musician evoking from a concert of artists the triumph of a master, is impersonal. Not by its aid did shepherds, one night, while watching their flocks, delude themselves with the wild notion that the stars had good tidings for them. Let us agree that the little box will do what the amateur at the piano could never do. Our ration of music, good and bad, now comes in from the main like our supply of water. We turn a button, and it is there. Nor has anything to be done for it; it is as certain as the income-tax. It also enlarges, on occasion, the voices of kings, premiers, and presidents. When they desire an urgent word with us they have a means to hand which the angels did not use because it was not there. They have that advantage over the angels. That new ability of the great and important to communicate directly with us is a bond between them and the humble. The King speaks in the kitchen. It is very agreeable for a household to be advised by the august voice of the Premier. Still, though while we sit at our fireside, listening-in after supper, flattered to hear a chief of state assure us that so far the likelihood of war next morning need not keep us awake, yet we certainly know that St. Michael, if ever he overcame the incoherence of the atmosphere, would not have an earthly chance. St. Michael cannot compete with a Chancellor of the Exchequer. If he tried to get a word through to us we should recognize at once an improper interruption; for we know well enough, we know it instinctively and sorrowfully, that the message he had for us, if any, would not come that way; it would be a personal word.

A personal word! Nobody else would hear it; nor might another fellow believe it if we reported a voice from beyond. But the radio is impersonal, and therefore it is right. Everybody but the deaf may hear it. It makes announcements as valid as the public notices once less effectively posted outside town halls, or left to the public press to issue. It has no heart. It is common news. It is not an intimation. It tells us that we are to be taxed a little more or less, or that, luckily, we may not have to shoulder arms for a month or two. What we hear is a louder speaker in the hurly-burly; the confused uproar becomes articulate, for a moment, with a pleasing assurance that the steep place is a little less steep, and that for the time being the herd is not rushing down. Which is gratifying enough; yet once I met a man who casually remembered, while lighting his pipe, that he used to know an ancient who had shaken hands with Beethoven. What, did the gods once live? Were they seen? Is it possible that this earth is habitable, for gods?

I went to the Talkies. It is no good trying to resist. We must accept the improvements on life made by machinery. The engine, we are aware, is dominant, and it rules us. We must submit to its governance. It has deposed Jehovah. It is the new God, the latest thing made out of our highest thoughts, and it must be worshipped, or the priests will certainly excommunicate us, and make our ways hard.

My town, quite near to London, of late has added to its many new buildings a palace for the

119

drama of the cinematograph. Once upon a time we had several theatres and music-halls, rather old and shabby places, and to these we went, following the ways of the people of old Athens, to see the life which puzzled us interpreted by a chosen company of cleverer fellow mortals; but the camera has dispossessed us. Those shabby old places have gone, outdated, mere memories now not kept by our children.

The magnitude of this new place, which we have in their stead, was astonishing. In central London, not Shakespeare and Handel and Wagner, not all the minds of the first magnitude, could keep it open for a profitable month. Yet what does that matter? For evidently the camera and the talking machine can do it. Its vast space was filled that night, though not, so far as I could see, with my neighbours. I could not see what had filled it, though full it was; its dim gulfs were uneasy with a stirring and a muttering, as of a tide in the dark. Sitting near me in an immense and dubious gloom I thought I recognized human shapes, a fond hope which had little comfort, because those shapes merged at no distance into an obscure mass which was awful in its sameness, extent, and ambiguity. That uncertain murk was not of men and women. A doubt came that

"... *and ranged on either hand were vague
masks, something human-like*"

this modern palace, where science employed its
devices upon an unknown quantity, might be a
station for charging a mysterious and inordinate
power, latent there for Heaven knew what. For
the power had no eyes and no voice. It was only
a murmuring and a stirring, as of a wind at sea
at night. If the wind should rise!

I suppose I was in a gallery. My feeling was
that I was suspended in midair with a multitude
of unauthentic beings. There were coloured au-
roral glowings on bastions and far rafters of
night, but they did not illuminate. They had no
apparent origin; there was but a spectral waxing
and waning of colours which did not throw light
on any complete and reasonable shape. Below
me was a twilight steep of which I knew nothing but a whispering and movement in the abyss;
and ranged on either hand were vague masks,
something human-like, that were lost in infinity,
that continued, I fancied, into the ultimate dark.
I prepared myself for a portentous and demonic
drama. I felt sure it would be that; I should get
no humane communication there. But there was
a bare chance I was not absolutely sundered from
my own sort, because I had a suspicion that one
of the bodiless spectres near me, one of the hover-
ing masks, was chewing peppermint.

A curtain rose, remotely and below, on the diminished simulacrum of a lighted stage. A company of acrobatic puppets appeared, and these dolls contorted their bodies to entertain us, while we waited for the greater shadow show to begin. On a vaudeville stage of the past such agility would have won applause. I heard no applause there. Perhaps spectres do not applaud puppets. The murk about me was silent. What was there to applaud? Puppets are not of flesh and blood; those figures were too distant to have backbones and bowels, so why should they not twist their bodies in a way impossible to a man? They were not cheered. They vanished. Other puppets came and sang mechanically or played musical instruments with a virtuosity remarkable in dummies; and they also departed in silence.

The smell of peppermint still reminded me of old earth, and I was glad it did, for I felt alone, and more than a little disquieted by this vast unreality. Unreal? How could one be sure it was not moved inimically by laws that concerned the asteroids and Saturn, but not the meek at heart? The immensity of this interior, which I could only surmise, the murmuring of the power which was phantom but potent, and that glowing upon detached bastions and cornices of undivulged lights, were too suggestive of the mechanistic compulsion which directs the multitudes in modern cities into uniform herds, orienting heads and tails according to influences from an inscrutable Zodiac. A boisterous if drunken laugh down below, a shout of ribald gaiety, would have been a godsend. I could have rejoiced in the knowledge of another lost mortal soul.

There was a pause. I was about to experience this new miracle of science, this shadow show with a voice. A magic lantern threw on a white screen lengthy indications of a great affair to come, and of its official sanction by the state censor, and portraits of the shadows who were "featuring," and solemn pauses which gave me time to read the meanings of sentences in a two-syllabic jargon for which a child at school would be reproved. The Talkie began.

It was my first and last. I judged that the masks and spectres about me might more usefully and amusingly haunt graveyards, than hover silently at this kind of entertainment. I used to think that the producers of the Movies had learned, after many trials, the limitations of their art. They knew the best use to make of their material. They had almost reached the point—

125

Charlie Chaplin reached it very quickly—where they would have seen that the power of the cinematograph was in the allegorical presentation of life. The magic lantern was taking its place with music and poetry. It could do what a great poem, we will say the *Inferno*, could not do. It could appeal directly to the multitude, and almost instantaneously, with an interpretative vision of man's affairs simple enough for all to understand and as immune from argument as the *Pilgrim's Progress*. It could persuade observers to a change of heart by a casual display of incidents in the life of the humble, which were of destiny and inevitable. The cinematograph, in the hands of imaginative genius, could have excelled poetry in its direct challenge to the ugliness in our institutions and traditional rites and manners; and that it was silent was the secret of its power.

But the spell of a symbol is broken when a bore explains what it means. The story conveyed by the Talkie in that immense and expensive palace was barely strong enough to support one number of an old-fashioned penny novelette. It concerned a despised singer who was loved by no one but his mother. She thought he could sing, but nobody else who knew him thought so. We might, in the silent drama, have assumed his loving mother was right, yet that night, most indiscreetly, he sang to us. We could hear that his mother was misinformed. We could plainly hear her dismal error, a nasal chant out of a Californiar tin. In one of the shabby music-halls of the past the soloist would have "got the bird" for making that noise. It is certain, however, that the manager of such a place would never have permitted him a nearer approach to the footlights than the cab-rank. The fable was so strangely foolish that it might have been conceived and produced by a simple-minded reader inspired by the serial stories which are proper to the cheaper picture-papers; the artless child would have supposed that to be the kind of thing the public wants. Its sentimental tedium was as slow as a leak of heavy stuff. Maybe, however, it was the work of an educated and ambitious South Sea Islander, after a close study of the missionary lady's more luscious magazines. He had attempted a contribution to English literature, and this was it. Our theatres have been diminished, our music-halls retired, and Charlie Chaplin advised that he is out of date, and the latest mechanism from the physical laboratories secured by men with too much money, in order that we should be gratified in a spacious new building by

Marie Lloyd, though gifted with the complete art of femininity, would be getting on; I remember thinking, that night, while waiting for her, that I must be all too late for her full charm; I was expecting too much. A lanky figure in a diminutive bowler hat, his trousers too short, his loose hands and wrists dangling well beyond his coat sleeves, with a cane, and a red nose, appeared on the platform. He tottered round it in agitation twice, and then stopped to inform us that his wife had gone away with the lodger. He made a song about it. Nobody present seemed to suffer very much, perhaps because they had heard something like it before. Another man followed, and jeopardized a number of dinner plates. Then a kilted figure appeared, whose recommendation was his Scotch accent; that is the only suggestion I can offer. The audience maintained its amiability.

There was some hesitation on the part of the management—the stage remained empty too long, while the audience murmured in its expectancy and a growing impatience. Then an electric number 10 suddenly flashed beside the proscenium.

The audience stirred, became quiet, and settled itself. The orchestra played an air which everybody but myself appeared to know well. Interrupting the music, a woman, wearing a dress that was an absurd caricature of the raiment supposed to appertain to a naughty lady, paraded insolently to the footlights. She only looked at us, in handsome weariness. There was a merry call from the gods. She sang a song in careless confidence, a little hoarsely, making hardly a movement, except of a shapely arm and an eloquent hand; sometimes there was a show of an ankle, which a woman might give who could do more, but merely wishes to annoy us. This was Marie Lloyd. Nothing was certain about her then except that my neighbours were fully under her control. She knew them, but she was as indifferent as a sultana in a tedious court. She lifted slightly her cloud of silk, mocked us with the prelude to a dance, and abruptly left us, with a grace that was contumelious. Just as she reached the wings she turned her head and gave us a look.

The immediate cry of delight which greeted the empty stage did not take me unaware. It is possible that I was in it. It is not easy to be dumb when taken by a glad surprise. If this was elderly Marie Lloyd, then she was eternal youth. Age she would never know . . . but was this all? For she could do more than this. Would she come again?

We could wait. It was far from midnight; or next morning would not be too late.

She appeared again, but I was not prepared for her. I knew at once I had not seen her before. Who was she now? A little shabby London woman, whose household was flitting, and somehow she had taken the wrong road. She had been following the van, but had lost it. She was carrying the family canary in a cage, and a handbag. She was tired, too, and I suspect she had been thirsty. She complained, in a droll way, in a language known to that house, of her tribulations. We laughed with her. What was she now? She was London. She was all the Cockneys. We laughed at ourselves.

Yet what is a Cockney? It is so hard to say that you will rarely find one in a book. There is Sam Weller, but not enough in literature to give Sam adequate companionship. The Cockney is a dangerous subject, who betrays most artists and authors. He is nearly as old as the Chinaman, and is something like that fellow, because of the antiquity of his civilization and its stress. He has worked for two thousand years, and still works, so he does not expect much. He is a hereditary unbeliever. He resists conversion to a new faith; the gods have upset his apple-barrow too often.

131

He has seen the death of many kings, and of so many great causes that he thinks it enough if he can keep his own barrow on two wheels for one day. He is sentimental, but protects his easy pity with a dry derision. He wears the mask of a cynic, and comments on affairs through restrained lips. Things have so often gone awry for him, notwithstanding the laws and the prophets, that it has ceased to be amusing; but this has given him patience, and his philosophy a bleak humour. He loves his fellow men, but he has no faith in them; he has seen too many of them, and too much.

How did Marie Lloyd convey this, and more? Well, how did Dickens manage it? And how often has Dickens been born again? Marie Lloyd, somehow, held communion with us. She did not have to speak. When she assumed that we knew, most certainly we knew, and chuckled. As a Cockney lady who had lost the van conveying her household goods, which was a grievous thing, though not without its fun, she would hesitate in an explanation of the accident, tongue-tied, and at once our sympathy flowed. Or she would, failing in her tired state to understand what it was she really wanted to do, ask us an innocent and irrelevant question. It was our own moving

job that was lost. But when she came, not to the
fine points of conduct, such as the way one may
innocently behave after several calls on a dry
road in the hope of conjuring up a heart re-
freshed, but to the elements of life, Marie
Lloyd's deranging candour would have moved
Sir John Falstaff to one of his grand and moving
periods. Her sallies shocked the house into wonder as deep as silence, just before it shook with
laughter. We had heard the truth, and knew it
almost at once. We understood each other better,
as we went home.

But here was this new great palace, and a new
age, and The Talkies. Now we are separate in
heart, though our bodies are herded; not Lon-
doners, Cockneys no more; we are the mob,
through the irresistible magic of another machine. Science assembles us, art does not unite us.
Influences that in a new jargon are called
mergers and syndicates have deprived us of con-
tact with the artist. We gape, and hardly know
why, at a distant and bloodless wonder. We have
grown distrustful of what is within ourselves;
for that, we have learned, is no longer of importance. Space and science insulate us from the
sympathy of humane communications. And there
is no compensation for our loss. Our ways of life,

under the compulsion of mechanical powers with which it would be useless to argue—they have no heads, as kings had, to be cut off—are shaping us into flocks with the same faces, the same wool, and the same desires. Our heads instinctively turn in one direction. We are losing our personal oddities and characteristics, for these are of no use, and are even dangerous to taskmasters. It is becoming hard to tell one sheep from another. We read the same newspapers, are prompted by the same loudspeakers, dance to the same music, and stampede before decisions not our own. There may be more than we think in that myth of the Gorgon's head; but instead of into stone its modern victims are changed into mutton.

❡The Dawn of Reason

It should not be supposed, because I shall mention Moscow, that I feel able to explain the effect of revolution on life and work in Russia. I do not know everything of Russia as it is, even though I have not been there. It would be wrong to make the high claim to plenary inspiration in a matter because of the strength of my moral perceptions, especially as I doubt that I have the gift to acquire knowledge through divination. All I will do is to assume that probably the effect of civil war and absolutism on a country is not pleasant, for it has been observed that a treatment of continuous violence to no more than a plot of grass will do it no good. Then again, we have been sufficiently warned, by lessons it would be hard to forget, that however pure may be our idealistic emotion wakened by an important event, that event, nevertheless, has its undesigned issues, and obeys its destiny regardless of the motives of its pioneers, and comes to an inevitable end unwelcomed because unforeseen by the lofty idealists who expected instead milk and honey in a happy valley secured from trespass.

It is safe today to write the name of Leon Trotsky, because the Russian Revolution has de-

clared that stalwart son to be illegitimate, and has
cast him out. Mr. Trotsky now would be less
safe in Moscow than you or I; yet as an amateur
general he so commanded the Red Army that he
made the Tsar's professional officers, when they
were aided by all that England and France dared
to give them, appear to lose battles by force of
habit. I think he must be a most intelligent and
formidable man, but it is safe now to name him
aloud, because Russia, whose revolution he saved,
disowns him. History seems to teach us that in a
revolution the men from whom we may expect
neither reason nor quarter are our comrades. As
we are secure in the knowledge that he is dis-
owned because of his defection in an article of
revolutionary faith too refined for outsiders to
perceive, we may freely examine Mr. Trotsky's
book on *Literature and Revolution.*

Should we doubt that our world cannot be better than what we commonly think and do, then
let us consider the excursion of this implacable
revolutionist into the realm of art. Mr. Trotsky,
after turning Imperial palaces into committee
rooms for the scientific discussion of democratic
needs, after abolishing with superb ease the
armies of those who would have restored the

Winter Palace to its traditional use, is at last free to give some attention to the poets.

That, we know, is more than the Tsar ever did. I do not remember that a crowned head ever published its reflections on the relations between literature and the state. The august guardians of a national constitution long and securely established may afford to neglect the poets, and probably not even a Poet Laureate would deny that. Poets may be tolerated and may win admiration, if not too queer; they are even encouraged, when their songs inspire popular thanksgiving for national virtues; yet always, at the back of our thoughts, is a little friendly contempt for the usual indifference shown by that genus for practical affairs. The artist is unable to cope, as a rule, with the coarse realities of the street, the mart, and the senate, though for rightly balanced minds which accept the world as it is, to make the most of it—and such we know our minds to be—the profitable management of those realities is not only native, but affords both interest and fun. Those remorseless facts are not funny to the poet, however, and that makes him, in private, funny to us. He is such a fool, and we enjoy the comedy his astonished innocence affords. Yet, in secret still, we are occasionally a little afraid of him. He can make us angry. We are aware of a certain demonic quality he has, which enables him to regard our comforting conventions and circumstances, that are as divinely based, we have no doubt, as the eternal hills, with eyes either unseeing or scornful. Does he see something we do not? For we have learned that, when his interest is lively, he is able to place things in the due order of their importance, by a careless inspection, while we are still puzzling over them, suspecting that here a choice of vital consequence is offered to us, yet unable to see where and why. And though we smile at his innocence, we have reason to dread his questions, as we dread the artless examination of a child who is suddenly curious about problems withheld from its nascent understanding. At times we are not certain whether we are listening to the silly prattling of an infant, or to the diabolic irony of a deathless spirit which looks like a baby but is older than Adam. We can remain certain of ourselves and our communal customs and rites only so long as the secret is kept of the skeleton in the cupboard. Does the child know of the old bones that are hidden by a door never opened? We doubt something unfortunate is there, for such is the traditional whisper, but we have never ventured a

"... a grinning skull might ask us in a
bony voice to distinguish between
truth and evil"

peep at that hidden thing. We do not care to look closely at the stuff we are made of. We do not seek trouble. There is no telling but what a grinning skull might ask us in a bony voice to distinguish between truth and evil, and we are not going to fashion an answer, if we can avoid it, for there is no guessing what would be involved. Beyond doubt it is better to maintain our cheerful and wholesome ignorance of questions that might test the props of society, for thus we may save the city we love from tumbling down. But how much does the blue-eyed infant and the poet suspect of what is behind our confident pomp and posture? Whatever they may guess, we will not confess one word beyond the point where the fine show of things, which gives us what we want, would be disturbed. If necessary we must lie to the child; there will be fairy tales so long as it is desired the young should accept as of divine ordination, or by inexorable law, that proper world which we maintain for them. As for the poet, with his inclination to upset the idols, we can keep him moderately suppressed on a low dietary; and as a rule we do.

Even Leon Trotsky sees that this is necessary. The Tsar and his court have gone, not before a change was highly desirable, and the Communists have come, but the poet is not abolished. Mr. Trotsky, with a quick instinct for any danger that may threaten that new society established by a revolution, turns to frown on the poet. He appears to know where trouble may begin. The poets helped the rebels to bring about that deep dislike of the law and order necessary to support Imperial Guards and Cossacks with knouts. The poet was not an anarchist. He was a poet. If he were in revolt, it was not against the Tsar, but ugliness. By the only light he knew, his country was an unhappy prospect, and he sang his protest to so good a tune that common people, who did not think their hard lot was known, or that anyone would care if it were, paused to listen, and were encouraged. The singer hints of a better clime, where we would fear winter less. He can change the look of things, turn even the sombre aspect of irrevocable fate into the shadow of human folly, which good will could disperse. When this is done, anything may happen, though the poet does not care; the rest is our concern. He scatters his words broadcast, and most fall on stony ground, but some do not.

In the beginning, we have been told, was the Word. How potent was the word! So let us never despise the idle singer of an empty day; his idleness may fill it, Heaven knows how. Perhaps Mr. Trotsky, when at leisure he began to consider the poets, remembered the words of such men as Tolstoy, Chekhov, and Gogol, pollenating stuff blown over the wilderness. He would have remembered, too, that all the Tsar's Cossacks could do nothing to subdue that magic.

From the tone of this book on literature by a revolutionary leader one would guess that he feels, about poetry, just what the Tsar's advisers used to feel. I do not think I should care to discuss literature in Moscow, any more than I should plead the loveliness of gentle peace in the smoking-room of a Pall Mall club, or the right to liberty of conscience in modern Rome. It would be inappropriate, and it might be dangerous. To discuss poetry with Mr. Trotsky would be as useful as reciting the *Ancient Mariner* while inside a tank in action. Not only would one's style be somewhat cramped, but one might not be heard.

If I were pressed, I should have to confess there is very much in literature I do not know and shall never learn. Our days are short and there is much to do. Yet, as to literature when a revolution is placing its machine guns in advantageous bedrooms at road junctions, we need be in no doubt whatever. It goes into the gutter. As do the babies, it dies, with much else that is good. Mr. Trotsky himself noted this, but it gives him no lasting remorse. With an original program that had destruction for its purpose, naturally he destroyed. Did poetry perish? No matter. It was only bourgeois literature. That properly went, with the society it flattered.

Still, Mr. Trotsky is intelligent and has read widely. He is aware of poetry. It exists. He rebukes his triumphant proletarian soldiers, therefore, when they complain that their own art differs from that of a despised and abolished group of time-servers, and when they beg of their great leader, "Give us something even pockmarked, but our own." He reminds them truly that a pockmarked art is not art, so is not necessary for the working classes. What Mr. Trotsky has to consider, in consequence, among the other duties of a revolutionist, is the proletarian production of poetry without pockmarks.

This product is not supplied in sunny abundance, even to the order of a revolutionary tribunal. And is there any pastime so interesting as watching a fanatic making recalcitrant facts accord with his faith? They ought to fit into his scheme, which he knows is right, and therefore they do, for they must. The process of reasoning, which is man's prerogative, can be no less wonderful than the life cycle of the liver fluke. Perhaps there is not a wonder of creation to equal it. It can reach the certainty of a moral conviction, by force of logic, with a celerity which makes man's evolution from a lemuroid shape seem a long, clumsy, and a very casual affair, hardly worthy the name of wonderful. Reason, in its humbler mood, pretends that it cannot square the circle; but it can do harder things than that; it can prove the circle to be a square, relatively, when considered with impartiality, should that be necessary to perfect a theory about which it feels ecstatic.

Because of this, Mr. Trotsky has few hesitancies when he looks to the future, to discern there the rise of proletarian art. Why should any man hesitate, when he is merely prophetic? He is supported, too, by the Marxian gospel, which has some of the advantages that jargon bestows on those who use it. Why not use it? If jargon cannot be depended on to do whatever a true disciple desires, what is the good of it? It is jargon which enables a Marxian revolutionist to be as reasonable as the Holy Office used to be when explaining that the execution of Indian infants after baptism saved them from further sin; as reasonable as Signor Mussolini when explaining that the imprisonment of political opponents brings an argument to the conclusion he desires.

In the first chapter of Mr. Trotsky's adventure in æsthetics there is expressed so savage a satisfaction at the discomfiture of poets, laughter so genial over their surprise at the withdrawal from their feet of the accepted earth, that one fancies one can hear an echo of the joyous shout which went up long ago when a ridiculous Christian toppled to a lion. He remarks, "the traditional identification of poet and prophet is acceptable only in the sense that the poet is as slow in reflecting his epoch as the prophet. If there are poets who can be said to be ahead of their time, it is because they have expressed certain demands of social evolution not quite as slowly as the rest of their kind."

So he cannot find a use for poets. They may sing their songs before sunrise, but not after. Let Juggernaut go over them. The revolutionist supposes, we see, that the poet should reflect his epoch, just as good Englishmen used to suppose that, to earn his guineas and his cask of wine, the Poet Laureate should celebrate the throne and exalt the Empire's flag. The trouble with the poet is that he will see us all damned first, revo-lutionists included. We have our hope and faith here; the topless towers of Ilium are of a dream which the light of common day never shows. Our world and the artist's cannot be reconciled; yet it will be perenially easy for Trotsky or another to parade the poets at dawn, and shoot them. They do not celebrate their epoch. As the gun-carriages go lumbering off to glory, we must not be astonished, nor grieve, when the Grecian Urn goes under the hooves and the wheels. It does not celebrate its epoch. And the devoted gunners, sure of the approval of patriotic onlookers, will merely turn in their seats to grin over their shoul-ders at the shards they have made. Something that was beautiful is lost. The gunners are amused. The populace is cheering too heartily to see that victory has already begun, and that the first death is on the road. But to what triumph in a new epoch does the Urn, now shattered, bear testimony? What is celebrated by its loss?

❧ The Gift

I was in Bridgeworthy again last week. There had been a call to a neighbouring town, and, when that was answered, I thought it would be pleasant to make a sentimental journey by carrier's cart to Bridgeworthy, six miles away. It would have been easier to go by train, though not better. I chose the traditional cart because that was how I first got into Bridgeworthy, and because it was said that in a few days a motor-bus would take its place; besides, old Gollop, most surprisingly, was still driving the cart. His large round face, red and convincing, with its circumference of misty hair, vague as a nimbus round the sun, regarded me with a November expression. He did not recognise me. He was unpleasant too, with his leisurely beasts; maybe he was thinking of that motor-bus, now so close behind us. I had to remember that this was one of his last journeys. It would have been wrong to have expected him to be as cheerily talkative as he was in the past. Indeed, he said nothing to me at all except, "Gonnochange."

Perhaps the motor-bus will not afflict Bridgeworthy with too many emendations. That is not my reasonable expectation, but a pious hope. Its

148

street along the river, it was heartening to see, was hardly different from what it was when first I saw it. There is now a war memorial, for one little change, and a picture palace, as stucco in an Oriental style is called, where the Jacobean ferry office used to stand. No, not exactly as I saw it first, for the first sight of it was on a serene day of June, when the pale houses, and the blue tidal river, were dilated in an early clarity of morning. Last week even the sky had a darkened light, the town was grey, and I will not say my own mood was much less critical than old Gollop's. This was a winter visit, with the wind northwest. We see things not as they are, but as we are ourselves.

I rebuked myself with that reminder; the difficulty is, though we think we ought to applaud progress, we hate change. It was pleasing, therefore, to see the same names over the shops. That confirmed the permanence of the base of the town. It would take something more than national progress, it was pleasant to suppose, to move ancient Bridgeworthy a serious distance. That thought was a good substitute for sunny weather. There still was the tobacco shop with its bow window, and the same blisters on its paint of black antiquity, where two of us filled our pouches in a hurry on our way to the London train, when we were returning to France. The same leisurely deacon filled my pouch again, out of a blue jar, with what appeared to be the same stuff. Smelling that mixture, while looking over the shelves of the bookshop next door, was almost startling. My tobacco smoke, for a moment, made me feel as though I had been spirited back past the clock a few years. But a sight of one of the latest novels synchronized me instantly with the current calendar. I retreated from what was latest; but, outside the bookshop again, what should I do to restore Bridgeworthy to a summer that was gone?

I remembered Mr. Falkland. Was he still there? Not much would have changed essentially if he were still in Limekiln Lane, to talk of Traherne. But the hope was faint. That Nonconformist parson, who read the mystics, yet considered Rabelais and Tristram Shandy to be nearer the right spirit than an Early Father or two, would be getting on. I could confess to the old man, if I could find him. When last we saw him we had thrown him into a little trepidation with some rebellious social opinions, not displayed by us in the best of polished manners, I am afraid, because we were so sure we were

right; youth grows vigorous with impatience
over the objections with which elderly sagacity
fuddles the straight and simple way to the truth.
He had told us then that London had fevered
us. We should never, he advised us, take truth
by assault. We ought to live in Bridgeworthy, so
that light and quiet might give us a long and
steady perspective. He himself seemed quite resigned, much too resigned I thought then, to the
tyranny of material things, and he was merely
amused by our supposition that anyone could get
near the truth in politics. He might be still in
the town, I dared to hope, for in Bridgeworthy
old speech and traditional ways were stubborn.
The town might have treasured him because he
was as native to it as the stones of its quay.

There was his church, and I examined its no-
tice-book. That church, that curious Gothic
fraud, persisted, but a new name was announced
in bright gilt on the board. Somebody named
Dudgeon. Falkland had gone.

I went round to the Royal Hart Inn, to wait
there for the train. The head of the stag over
the dining-room door was as dusty as it used to
be. The bell-pulls, too, were the old deer-hooves.
George, the waiter, was still standing in the
empty dining-room, looking over the river, as I

entered, and he merely raised his eyebrows and put his head sideways, in salutation. From the way he spoke, he might only have missed seeing me since yesterday, because that was a wet day.

The landlady, I found, was the one I used to know, but she had married again. The new host was a large and genial soul, and we were the only three to lunch there. I heard of all the changes, except one, for the landlord was pleased to discuss them. His buxom wife, with hard black eyes to match a necklace of jet, was superior to our conversation, and took no part in it. Presently I enquired after the welfare of Mr. Falkland.

The landlady spoke for the first time. "He's gone," she said, with noticeable emphasis. The Royal Hart Inn had been always faithful to Mr. Falkland's Church. The landlord chuckled. His wife, though, was not at all amused. Had there been a scandal, I wondered? An absurd and improper thought!

The landlord laughed at me. "He was kicked out," he explained.

"Don't talk like that," his wife ordered. She flushed, and her eyes were severe. She turned to me. "We had to ask for his resignation."

"Why," I cried in astonishment, "what had he done?" It occurred to me that Falkland him-

self had told me, though that was years ago, of
a church meeting to come when he was to be
presented with something or other. I mentioned
this to the landlady. "I thought he was so popular."

"So he was. But he did for himself."

The landlord, indifferent to the glistening jet,
did not control his diversion over my innocent
wonder. "That's what did it," he explained.
"That present. That's what did it."

The landlord did not glance at his wife's eyes.
Something funny had taken his fancy. He was
enjoying himself. He laughed deeply again. "A
microscope! That's what they gave him. He
asked for it. Ever heard of a man going to the
dogs over a microscope? I couldn't do it, could
you?"

"It's no business of yours, Henry," said the
landlady. "It was nothing to do with you. You
never knew Mr. Falkland."

"Not me," remarked her husband, cheerfully.
"Not me. I wish I had. He must have been a
queer old bird. I'm sure I should have liked
him."

"Very possibly." She addressed herself, though
with dignity, to her serious guest. "How it
happened," she said to me, "I don't know. Who

suggested a microscope, a thing like that, for a minister, I never asked. He may have asked for it himself. I expect he did."

"Doesn't seem more naughty than some things I've heard tell of," the landlord commented.

"I don't know what you may have heard tell of. Let me speak. He had the thing, in any case. What he used to study with it I can't say, though we began to hear a lot about it in his sermons afterwards. There were complaints long before we had to go and see him. Letting tadpoles loose in the gospels! Then came the day when some of us went to interview him about the young girl who was organist . . ."

"Nothing to do with the microscope, that," the landlord interrupted. "Though a pretty bit of goods she was."

His wife paused for some patient but ominous seconds, while the landlord examined his tankard. "Pretty? Taking enough, I dare say. But I thought it was me who was explaining what happened. As I was saying, we went to see him about that girl. We had to go then, though it was too late. There was the church to think of. She had to go. And what did we get out of the man who ought to have been most concerned for the good name of the church? All we could get out of him

154

". . . that's what did it"

was shaking his head. He said it was very sad. And was the girl in distress? That was what he was anxious about. That! What we felt, what the church would suffer, didn't matter to him. He said he would think about it—you'd have thought we were just common busybodies. If he wasn't just trying to put us off I don't know what you'd call it. He spoke of other things. 'Before you go,' he said to me, 'come and look at this.' You may believe me, or believe me not, but he walked over to that microscope. It was on a table. I will say I think the man must have been crazy."

"Don't you believe it. He was only artful," said the landlord.

"Then I'll take your word for it. Artful, was he! Well, I walked over with him, not thinking at first he meant that brass thing. Who would? But he told me to look through it, and like a fool I did. I was that flustered I didn't know what I was doing. And just before we all left him . . ."

"But pardon me," I broke in, "do tell me what you saw in it?"

"Nothing. Only a lot of very bright colours. The sort of thing you see in that thing children play with—yes, kaleidoscope. Falkland turned a screw or button, and the colours all changed. Like a child! He told me it was a bit of the rock on which Bridgeworthy was built, though how should I know it was? I still say he was crazy. What do you think he said to me then? This is what he said. 'Now you've seen what a beautiful earth ours is. Even Bridgeworthy is built on a rainbow.' Then he walked over to the window and looked out. He turned round in a minute, and spoke to me, as if I were the worst of the lot. I don't know why he spoke to me. There were four other women. 'If we could only see that child's fault as we see what bright stuff even our old town is built on, we might not be so sure of our own righteousness.'

"That," continued the landlady, calmly, after a pause, "was more than I could stand."

"I reckon it was," agreed her husband.

"I went for him, straight out. 'So you'd make a rainbow of sin, would you, Mr. Falkland?' I said. Just like that. He looked very hurt. I meant him to feel it. Nice thing for a minister to suggest to a mother, wasn't it?'"

"How did he take it when he was asked to resign?" I enquired.

"Well, he heard all about it at the church meeting. He sat looking at the floor, smiling a little. When it came to his turn to speak, he merely shook his head, stood up, and was walking out of the vestry. But he stopped at the door, and said, 'I have served you many years, but now I am beginning to learn my work here I must go. I am very sorry.' Then out he went."

We were silent for a time. The landlord finished his tankard, and then said, "Well, Bill who ferried him over to the train told me that the old 'un had tears in his eyes as he crossed the water with his bag."

"It was a cold day," said his wife.

⟪The Changeling

The windows of the railway carriage were thickened with rain. I could see little of the country except the telegraph posts and wires unendingly rising and falling in flight beside the line. The book I was reading was as long as the journey. It was a volume of history: it was deliberate with quotations from state papers and the speeches and letters of puissant men, because its author intended that if I remained in ignorance of the evidence, then the blame should not be his. The book, coolly and without haste, attempted to unravel a tangle in the story of mankind, a tangle that was recent, one indeed which had had me in its knots, one that I was well aware could not be attributed to a cause so simple and fair as was Helen of Troy. My author's discreet purpose was that I should be deprived of the consolation of romance for so confused and evil an epoch; nevertheless, he could not help deepening my wonder over the strangeness of life.

The telegraph wire fled undulating past. There were still many hours to go. And this book, I must confess, was not sedative, though compelling. A reader's tidy mind was disordered by it. It fascinated him with a suggestion that,

though the laws of the great universe have no
concern with morality, which is a various impo-
sition of our own, yet somehow the conceits of
men of noble purpose, who would do good
by stealth, may bring down evil on us instead,
yet logically, out of the blue void which should
know not good nor evil. How does that happen?
I considered so unlucky a mystery, having
nothing else to do, while reading this history,
until the fear came that high life was a drama,
not of kings, courtiers, diplomats, statesmen, and
spies, but of phantoms, blind agents of what
could not be named, inscrutable and inimical
genii, moved by humane reasons to unholy strata-
gems, provoking an unintended crisis, all for our
good, from which we averted our faces in horror.
It was as baffling as a nightmare, in which fantastic logic moves the silent shadows to an in-
felicity which is both ridiculous and dire. I began
to feel I had read my book long enough.

My eye roved over my fellow passengers, who
were, I believe, commercial travellers. I was glad
of that. They were not historians or philosophers.
One of them was certainly free of troubled concern with the fateful moves of unsuspecting life.
I found his appearance quite heartening. After
all, the world had a number of such men, such

young men, large of limb, and superior with
health and cheerfulness. He was handsome and
blithe, and on a day of rain and wearying travel
was trying to keep fellow mortals amused by
trickery with cards. He was clever. He could do
things with them which were unexpected and absurd. He was not at all the sort of man to have
against you at the card-table. Presently he put
away the cards; they could do no more for us. He
enquired of one of the other men about a colleague, to be told that that colleague had met with
misfortune. I learned enough to know that somewhere in the background was a principal with a
hard face, who never could be convinced that
orders for merchandise are seldom given by cus-
tomers too poor to buy it.

The men laughed and smoked, indolent and
reminiscent, and told each other stories of various employers and their ways. As I listened,
for in good nature they addressed themselves to
me as well, I began to learn a little of the virtues
one had to acquire, when not inherited, for success on the road. It seemed to me, too, as I
watched them, that these worthy men would be
no more likely to regard in curiosity the unrav-
elling of the knots in the history I had been reading than if that human drama had been written

in hieroglyphics. They would not care. They were practical men, and dealt with measurable commodities. The dark of the mind, which occasionally gives the history of humanity the semblance of figures of moonshine compelled to bedevilment, was not obscure to them. Either it was not there, or at its worst it was only the conscious disguise of low cunning.

Then the talk veered to the strange people they had met when travelling. One of them remembered an old lady, who entered his compartment only last week and brought with her a small wheelbarrow, in which was a brown-paper parcel. She did not sit on a seat. She sat on her barrow, protecting her parcel with her person. The train moved on, and the old lady had composed herself. Our friend could not help noting her with some surprise, and she must have seen she was observed. She advised him that if he dared to talk any of his nonsense she would ring the alarm. His fancy conversation was not desired. She knew his sort. She had brought, she warned him, her own alarm, for she was too short to reach the apparatus provided for emergencies by the railway company. She put beside her on the seat in readiness her alarm, a bell for a restaurant table.

163

That amused us. Did he make her ring it? We found we had quite a collection of such oddities. We showed them to each other. There was the sinister fellow who manages to get in with you at night, when you are alone. There were others, not quite so common. The handsome young man, who had been so clever with a pack of cards, told us of a strange encounter he once had on a railway journey.

"Well, he was about the funniest old duck I've ever met. I've never been able to make out what his little game was. He made me rather nervous at first. You see, I'm blest if I know where he came from. I hadn't noticed him. That was the worst of it, for I do notice people. There he was, anyhow, in my compartment. How did he get there? Through a ventilator, if you like. He was crazy right enough.

"I've thought about him since. You listen to me. I want to know how he got in. What? Yes, of course. A corridor coach. We were on the move. No stop since Paddington, and I was the only one in the compartment, nobody else. And I happen to know that coach did not connect with the rest of the train, because I'd been along the corridor. I was in the end compartment, a

smoker. There were only about six people in the
carriage. Eh? Oh yes, we did stop at Reading,
but I noticed no change in the other compart-
ments, for I went along again. About six people
altogether, in the coach. I know what I'm talking
about.

"I was sitting with my feet up, smoking, when
I noticed this old chap for the first time. He was
in the corridor, staring into the next compartment. Nobody was in there, I knew. I was in it
a minute before, and got a newspaper I saw on
the seat. I had nothing to read. Only had just
time enough to get into the train. I didn't take
much notice of the man standing there. He had
no hat. His grey hair was rumpled. I thought he
seemed a bit anxious, as if he was looking for
some one, but nobody was in that compartment.
Then I forgot him.

"After a bit I heard a voice. 'Excuse me, sir.'
I looked up. Hullo! thinks I, an American. Anyhow, his clothes had a rum cut, his face was
smooth and pale, and he had a short grey mous-
tache. He had an angler's basket slung behind
him—hanging down by his side—what d'ye call
it?—a creel. That's right. I wondered what he
wanted that thing for. Sandwiches, perhaps. I

couldn't make out where he had been sitting. You could hardly miss such a chap."

"Well, he was there then, so he must have been there before," interrupted one of us.

"That's right. Only I always notice people, and I hadn't noticed him. I was going to say that he pushed into my compartment. Damned his own basket. It got in his way. He was very excited. He was trembling.

" 'Have you seen my luggage, sir?' he asked. But he didn't give me time to say no. He rattled on, without looking at me. 'But of course you haven't. Facing the engine, my corridor was on the left, and this one's on the right. This isn't the carriage. I don't know this carriage,' says the old chap. 'What shall I do?' he said.

"I didn't know what to say to him. I wished he'd go away. But he only went to the other window and looked out. Then he muttered to himself 'I suppose I must wait till I reach Doncaster.'

" 'What?' I said to him. 'Doncaster? This train doesn't go to Doncaster.'

"You should have seen that old fellow's face. I might have insulted him. He looked at me. At first he seemed angry, and then jolly miserable.

"*The old boy seemed paralysed with astonishment*"

He put his hands over his eyes. Then he looked at me again, and said, very quietly, 'Tell me, young man, when did we leave King's Cross?'

" 'Why,' I said to him, 'you ought to know that West of England trains don't go from King's Cross. We left Paddington about six.'

"That did it. That tore it. His jaw dropped. I could see by his face he was cracked, and I wondered what he would do next. But what surprised me was the way he controlled himself. 'Of course,' he said, putting his hand over his eyes again. 'Of course. Paddington.'

"I felt like laughing, but I thought I'd better not. Might touch him off. Then the old fellow bundled through the door again into the corridor, and was going away. But he came back and spoke to me. He was quite cool, but his face was twitching. 'I want to tell you, young man,' says he, 'that I did leave King's Cross, and I was going to York. You are lying. This train is lying. My clothes are lying. I don't know them. What does this basket mean? I don't want it. It isn't mine.'

"He was nodding slowly at me as he spoke. I didn't answer him. Thought it better not to. 'I tell you,' he went on, 'that I left my hat on the seat. Where is it? I left it on the seat when I went

169

forward to the dining-car to dinner. I know I did. Now I can't find it. I come back, and I can't find anything I know. I can't find even that dining-car now.'

"Nice position for me to be in, wasn't it?" said the young commercial. "I wished one of the other passengers would come along. But he seemed very quiet. Anyhow, the old boy looked a good deal more scared than I felt. He really did. Talked an awful lot, to try and convince me. He said he'd given the waiter sixpence, and that he'd know the man anywhere. He said he'd upset a bottle of dry ginger on the dinner-table. Little things like that. He seemed to be trying to remember them.

"When we stopped at Bath, the collector came for the tickets. My strange pal asked for the diner. He was told there wasn't one. Hadn't been. The collector asked again for his ticket. I think the collector had the idea that the poor old dear was trying to rush the company.

"The old boy seemed paralysed with astonishment. Said he'd give them his card, and all that. Pulled out his pocket-book. He looked at it, looked over at me, and whispered, 'It's not mine.' Then he flung a visting-card at me. 'I don't know him,' he cried. 'I was never in America, never there, never.'

"I've got that card now. It has a name, 'Otto R. Ralph.' Funny name, isn't it? They had some trouble in getting him out. I've often wondered what became of him."

ℂ Côte d'Or

If you look out in time, Dijon is a name on a railway station to be seen in France when you are going somewhere else. The first time I noticed it was at three in the morning, in January, 1914, when an abrupt jolting wakened me, and I was curious to learn how much nearer we were to Switzerland. Dijon then was but a group of French soldiers in cherry-coloured bloomers under a feeble lamp; then our train moved on. Dijon was of no significance.

The next time I was there we were kept in Dijon station a long time. Our train was on its way to Paris, and was itself crowded with soldiers —for now it was early in the September of 1914 —some with wounds which were evidently gangrenous; and if they were not wounded men, then they were weary fellows, in bloomers not so cherry-coloured as formerly, who were in no mood to talk of war, who had been fighting for weeks, and had been ordered, just as they were, to another battle-field. Some of us were twenty-four hours standing in a corridor of that train, in a smell I got to know rather better later on.

And this autumn, travelling in France again, I was reading a book, and had got to a point in

it where its author was assuring me that peace-
makers, however blessed otherwise, can never be
historians, when my train slowed, and stopped,
with a familiar jolt. Dijon! This time it was my
destination.

Well, whether it is impossible for an agnostic
to write fiction, or a Buddhist to write philosophy, or a Christian to write poetry, or a man who
is all for peace to write history, are doubts I do
not care to resolve; yet I did feel for a few minutes there in Dijon again, merely as a man who
sometimes thinks that peace has a few good
points, that history must be far from easy to
write. How could one get in everything? How
could one be as impersonal and as just as a seraph
who had to report to the Ineffable? It was foolish, of course, to glance along Dijon's platform
for the group of soldiers once glimpsed under a
weak lamp wearing a uniform now forgotten;
still, somehow the men of the war who are less
than nameless, who might never have been more
than shadows which became one with night when
their feeble lamp went out, were more real to me
than all the activity in that railway station of
the present.

Impossible for some of us to write history? I
should say it is. One had better call history the

least satisfactory department of biology, and leave it to anybody who is confident he recognises a fact when he sees it. It is no good going for facts to the sentimental who ponder what is invisible; they may confuse things. The trouble for such writers, if they attempt history, is that they will see humanity as men and women, and so stand in danger of getting hopelessly lost. You may write anything you please about the myth called humanity, and you are safe from mockery, because generalities concerning a myth are never funny; but once you begin on Tom, Dick, and Harry, you had better be careful. Those fellows wore trousers, and fell in love, had children, and on the day they were "called up" they went out to lonely corners to think it over. For them war meant separation, ruin, and the end, by all the odds. It was not for them a generality which only affected an abstraction called humanity. And we happen to remember a few of those fellows. How can they be omitted from history when history is nothing without them?

I do not know. But they are omitted. So history, to some of us, be it as august and wise as is possible while forgetful of the inhabitants of Dumdrum, is nothing; it is addressed to the reason and never to the bowels. It belongs to anthropology, that most romantically speculative subject, which changes its centre of interest with each psychological fashion, that is, once a year. Nevertheless, I am bound to confess that recently the ticket collector at Dijon station stood not in the autumn of 1914; he demanded a valid voucher, which I had taken the precaution to bring with me. That was lucky, for by the look of him I am sure that Frenchman knew nothing of a Dijon I could see. It was not on the map, much less on the line of the P.L.M.; so he allowed me to go in and out of another Dijon station just as I pleased; everybody's ticket for that place had been given up long ago, I suppose.

Then there was a lengthy automobile drive in the Côte d'Or towards a sunset of the autumn of this year. I suppose the French will never believe it of the English, because the French are given to logic and the English to sentiment, but there are many of us to whom much of France is the same as home. We passed that evening a hill on which stood one battlemented wall of an old castle; the rest of the castle was rubble and thicket. That was where in 1423 the Duke of Bedford, before Joan of Arc made him feel a bit less ducal, married Anne of Burgundy. Yet I do not mean such monuments as that; not anything of such historical note. But when day had nearly gone we passed the side of a common village home, a pale wall with an exclamation on it: Byrrh! You will know how I felt about it if ever you have been checked by an exploding shell when crawling amid ruins, and have looked up to see that heartfelt word confronting you on the only wall left upright in a French hamlet. Besides, the Côte d'Or is, geologically, a Dorset on a bolder plan; the hillsides which give us the best wine there is have the forms of those noble downs you see in the unfrequented England between Lulworth Cove northwest to Lyme Regis, and are built of similar rocks. Those limestones have the seal of an ammonite as a guaranty of their quality, and they weather as buffs and greys which shine, when they are waterworn, with the rich softness of nard; they tell you at a glance that this earth is ample and generous. When writing history, how is it all to be got in?

Then our car swerved into a hollow where the night was thicker in patches—probably here was another village—and it came to a stand by a shallow terrace above which was a large door with one small lamp. The oil lamp was humble and did not make much of the hall within; the night kept close around us. There was the smell of a

176

log fire. A broad staircase of stone went up from the hall, apparently to the invisible stars. It rested on darkness round a bend. A few old portraits seemed on the point of emerging from the gloom, at our entrance, but hesitated on the verge of distinction, perhaps shy of modern interlopers.

We were welcomed by an American and his lady. This was their house, though built before a revolution that had nothing to do with them; it was not their revolution. I held a candle up to one portrait; a shrewd and bearded face screwed its eyes down at me. The candlelight shone on a steel corslet. Messire François de la Plume! Seigneur there in 1580. The American in his tweeds gazed at François in his steel; but this little history is unable to record whatever may have passed between them, though I know it would be highly interesting to learn. Philadelphia now; but once it was François de la Plume, who was military governor of the fortress of Semur when Henri III was king of France, and Drake, on the English side, was just back from Ternate, and the Spanish Armada was getting into being. Besides, the son of these Americans flew for France in the last war, and long before his countrymen were in it, I fancy. So as to history, it seemed to me like that staircase, the bottom steps of which were obviously substantial, but they neared us out of impenetrable shadows from round a corner of night; you might think you could guess what was out of sight, but most likely the guess would be strangely wrong.

It has been my lot to get accustomed to several French châteaux, whether or not I liked their circumstances, but here for the first time my bed was provided with a canopy of crimson brocade fifteen feet high. Peace was in this house. I did not in the silence of this French house listen to distant guns, the mutterings of Ypres. In the outer dark now there was but the questioning notes of owls; and it was strange that the rapid evolutions of a bat, who was confused by my candle, should have been quite noiseless. The room was so large that after the bat had passed through the candle's utmost effort he was gone; the transits of the bat were swift, intermittent, and baffling. His shadow would pass over my history book like a hieroglyphic too brief in any case for deciphering; no easier to understand than the muttering of Ypres in the night.

I will not say it is possible for a lover of peace to write history, because that kind of man, like a pro-German, or a pro-Boer, an English baron, or a hundred-per-cent American, may be any-

" . . . *you were lost in the spacious quiet*
of it"

thing, even a rascal. He might write anything; he might pretend to be an ancestral voice prophesying war, at the right price. But in the morning I did wonder, looking from my window, which was above a moat where a shoal of carp were playing follow-my-leader over a stick, to where in a meadow under the Burgundy hills and the sun a herd of white cattle were grazing, whether any book worth the name can be done except by a mind at peace. I felt then that poetry, at least, is not likely to be given to men whose minds are at war with this or that. Perchance peace is not the absence of war, a mere certainty that for the present the ships and the railway trains continue on their schedules. The state of peace, perhaps, is but a personal matter, and for those who can attain to it the guns, should they go off, and the authority of the pro-consul's guard, do not count. I wondered that morning whether without the harmony which only a mind sure of its centre can bestow upon the perplexing prospects of earth, we are as likely to find great art justifying our cities as we are to chance upon Apollo managing a glue factory. In spite of Ruskin's assurance of the poetic inspiration of conflict, in which he is supported by the truculent critics of our own day who would have us believe that the real right fel-

lows are as curly-fronted bulls, lords of the cows
and the ranges, I doubt that our latter-day democratic need for gas-masks will move us in the way
the builders of the Gothic cathedrals and the
great musicians were moved. We greatly desire
great art to arise in our cities. We desire, in fact,
to have things both ways; to retain our glue
factory when it is so profitable, and with the glue
we want the flashing of the wheels of the chariot
of the sun. We would look up from the clangour
of our prosperous industry, in which we desperately hope to find peace and security, and expect
to find also the contributory poets standing atten-
tive while chanting the glory of our state to give
us heart. For we badly want encouragement; we
want the justification of our condition by the
bards as they celebrate its beauty. That would remove a lurking doubt we have.

The poets, unluckily, do not oblige us; not con-
vincingly; not even Whitman. We are beginning
to suspect that much of Whitman's celebration of
the Modern is bluff. Whitman bluffed himself.
He shouted himself down, deafening himself—
for he did not want to pause, even for a moment
—with lusty iteration of the naturalness of ugliness, of the native attraction of barbarities and
squalor, and the intimate hairiness of chests and

way of learning tolerance in the old place, where the only sound of life in the heat of noon is the undertone of unseen wings in the lofty aisles of its avenues of elms and limes, a sound that is an assurance, in the midst of still antiquity, of latent energies yet to be fulfilled: there is nothing actively patriotic in a mind given to reverence of what is lovely and of good report. To judge by the appearance of the suburbs of London, for motor roads, and houses as shrill as piercing screams, are destroying Surrey, and by the prospect of the eastern suburbs of Paris, where the horrors that arise in the development of the English countryside are even exceeded, we on our side of the Atlantic could no more be trusted with the guardianship of a corner like Salem, Mass., than any native incorporation of energetic realtors. The truth, I fear, is that ardent patriotism anywhere is shown in a pride which expresses itself, for the most part, in but an ugly, loud, continuous, and nonsensical noise; nations care less for their best achievements and traditions which belong to all the world, than they do for their Sunday newspapers and chickens. This château of an ancient line, a happy relic, was saved from falling into a hen-roost and a store for farm litter by an American; not because he is an American, but because he is more than that, and would cross China, if he could, to save the world from the loss of an item of rare porcelain. To him beauty is not national, but is the charge of whoever happens to know it.

In all its aspects created beauty is our chief justification before Heaven, and so its care is the charge of any man on whom light has fallen as a sign. That nation is the great nation where this sign of grace is most welcomed; but as yet that sign is nowhere welcomed as a national historical event so noteworthy that even a peacemaker could record it joyfully without reproof. I merely remark, therefore, that this American is also a citizen of the only country some of us now acknowledge as ours, a privilege he shares with many unknown soldiers who wore all the varieties of the steel hat; a country which never discusses the problem of disarming, for there is no anxiety about its frontiers, a country which has no premier or president to whom one of its people would give five minutes' attention, unless he had something to say; though I must admit that the tax it levies upon anyone willing to bear it is fairly heavy. It is not one of the new little countries which the late war released from bondage, though it is far more ancient than any Great Power, if not on the map. Its citizens know each other, when they chance to meet, but that is as much as you can say about them. They do not often meet.

There is an avenue of old trees leading up to the house in which the full day is but a greenish twilight. When the house is seen in sunlight beyond the framing end of the avenue, its front, of Caen limestone, looking to the south, seems self-luminous, and of the placid shine and colour of a newly risen harvest moon. The ridge of the steeply pitched tiles of the roof is as casual along the blue of the sky as an outcrop of coral rock, which frost has moulded, and the tiles, too precipitous for verdure, are immemorial with lichens. An artist had to build such a place, and it took two centuries to finish it, but its light is no less than the aura from the best that man has done on one of his more likely places under heaven. You get not only a surmise of his ancient establishment, which was long before Rome was built, or even Athens became possible, but you learn that, in spite of the energetic efforts of some of his kind towards a more efficient organization of his resources, which have seriously interrupted him, he has done rather well. If it is not possible to feel foolishly hopeful about him, yet in such a scene one may be tranquil. He has some good

things to go upon. He has been given a right lead,
if only he could happen on the clue to its whereabouts. If he wants it at any time, it exists for
him.

We know, as literary critics, and as critics of
much else, that it would be silly and softening
to consider the lilies. They make no effort. They
make no noise. If they are not noticed they do
not grieve. They merely are. It is possible they
do not worry even when their sweetness is wasted
on the desert air. It would be ridiculous to consider a virtue which merely is, and claims nothing, not even recognition. Such a virtue is no
better than the voice which was inattentive to its
business because it was still and small. A proper
instinct warns us to ignore such hints. If ever we
paused to consider whether something not altogether without importance was to be learned
from a sign that made no effort to attract our
attention, there is no telling but that things might
go hard with us. To give attention to a voice
which was so gentle it could not be heard, if one
preferred not to listen to it, but which, if the ear
were so inclined, could empty out the importance
of much that was loud and urgent, might have
grave consequences for us. We know that well
enough; but in the deadening uproar of our ever-

revolving machines we can be perfectly safe, and no harm can come to us. We can gravitate together into crowds, for moral support, and loudly cheer things in common for an assurance that we are doing well.

But in that ancient house in Burgundy one sadly felt, after reading a modern book sure of its popular appeal with its force and eloquence, a suggestion of amusement in the unaltered quiet and repose. Perhaps the place had heard all that before, and knew what had happened. The dangerous idea came that, by chance, you had wandered into another dimension. You were lost in the spacious quiet of it. You had better be wary. If you stayed there long enough you might find you had forgotten a way back to a world that had been left somewhere round the corner on another plane. How to return to safety? I was considering this, sitting on the stone terrace; and a moon, quite as you now suggest, began to play tricks with its beams about the old towers, and within the dim aisle opposite of tree-columns, and made me see things which have no existence for sane people; then something began to speak beside me.

I record but the literal truth. There was a voice. Nobody was there. No voice could be as small as that, either, nor as still. No bell, for the sound was bell-like, could be so minute. It sounded clearly enough, however, where the order of things was not quite right. There was no escape. The voice could not be ignored. I had to listen. The sound was so frail and musical that it could be heard only when the air had been emptied of sunlight and the head of serious thought. Fairies have been abolished; and time they were, too, because when there seems no escape from the control of matters of fact we can dispense with magic spells. I knew, indeed, that the music I heard was but the soliloquy of a small lizard. Yet if only our own words could be made light and simple enough to carry that music . . . though who would hear it except when the moon was at her tricks? How could one do work which was worth doing when back in Babel with this hungry generation, make an effort to translate into forthright deeds the eloquence of our major prophets, and the call to duty of a church militant, and the inspiration of our glorious history, if confused by such oblique hints?

❰Exploration

The repining began in me through reading Ballantyne's *Hudson's Bay*. The pull of the Magnetic North was felt; I turned to Boothia Felix. I should not like to say how long ago that was; it was when I began to have occasion, in a house of commerce, to consult the *Weekly Shipping List*. That entrancing guide contained such entries as this: "York Factory, Hudson's Bay. *Lady Head*, bk., 457 tons, A. I. Capt. Anderson. Sailing June 1. South West India Dock."

I was very young then, and so supposed a man went travelling to see what was round the corner; because, as a sage master mariner, later in life, once sadly explained to me in his cabin: When we are young we think all the good things are far away. I did not know, so early, that a man sets out to find himself, and that on such a journey, in a country all unknown, he may get lost. When young Herman Melville shipped in a whaler, he little guessed his voyage would never end, not while men fancy they discern a Great Bear in the night sky, from which their brave harpoons ever return to earth.

Ballantyne unsettled me, and Butler's *Great Lone Land*, and *Wild North Land* made matters

worse; it was the dream that was real. Lake Atha-
basca and the Mackenzie River were desolate;
and how noble were their names! But the Hudson's Bay Company, at whose door in Lime Street,
London, I knocked, generously spared my prof-
fered service. It amused me once to hear Joseph
Conrad confess—it was to my ear alone, and I
had made no confession to him—that his earliest
effort to find employment as a ship's officer was
with the H. B. C.; and he, too, failed, for the
H. B. C. is Scotch, and most careful and particular. There was not a book on the exploration of
North America and the Arctic, in the Guildhall
Library of the City of London, for which I did
not save or steal time to read. It came to nothing.
But the very name, Canadian Barren Grounds,
still works a faint reminiscent enchantment; yet
resolutely but regretfully I resist the Northern
Lights.

The ease with which a man may get into the
outer blue, which is uncharted, and is not at all
kenspeckled, I learned a little later, from *A Week
on the Concord*. Once you have started you may
find yourself anywhere. The transit may be instant. There is no oracle to warn you where you
may be at night. You may be so different that the
world itself will be changed. Then what will you

do?—for do something you must. When your
fellows continue as usual to call your burning bush
a briar patch, which is what it is, and will remain
for most of us, how is that sign to be doused?
There is no return.

There must be categories for books, yet I do
not think Books of Travel is precisely the place
in the index for the *Arabia Deserta*, or Thoreau's
Week on the Concord, or even for Bate's *Natural-
ist on the River Amazon*. The right good book is
always a book of travel; it is about a life's journey.
It does not matter whether the point of view is
got from Egdon Heath, Capri or Kanchenjunga.
The *Seven Pillars of Wisdom* was to me less Arabia in war time than Lawrence; the war and its
intrigues, the Arabs, the Turks, and the Germans
and the desert, were incidental; they chanced to
evoke Lawrence, agents of destiny of consequence
to us, for they were the cause of a war of thoughts
compared with which the desert campaign was
only ugly and common tribal bickering. Revolts
of Arabs and others against what enrages them
may burn up a little rubbish, and perhaps make
more, but a revolt from our traditions and accepted verities by bleakly intrepid thoughts may
lead us the deuce of an eternal dance. Is *Moby*

Dick a yarn of a whaling cruise? Is *Gulliver's Travels* merely a fantastic diversion?

We shall continue to call the *Arabia Deserta* a book of travel, for it is that, though so is the *Pilgrim's Progress*. Nevertheless, it is plain that Doughty, that gaunt and stubborn survival from a pre-Shakespearian England, so much an Englishman that he was a foreigner to the Oxford and London of his day, looms in his book with more startling distinction than the basaltic crags of the Arabian desert. No wonder his spirit held in check the sunstruck fanatics about him, though they wanted to cut his throat. We, too, were in nature as much opposed to him when we began to read him, but he has subdued us. The stark bergs of his desert are not more enduring than the traveller. But for him, would that burnt region of sand and rock with its dangerous and rhapsodical nomads exist for us? While reading Doughty, you begin to sense something of the origin of the Semitic scriptures; we know that Doughty himself, had he been one in the Exile, brooding on lost Jerusalem, would have bowed to the stripes, but have prophesied apart for all those that must hereafter patiently endure by the waters of Babylon.

First and last a poet may write only of himself. The world exists because he sees it. That can be all he knows of it. What then, is he? For the validity of the world depends on the kind of man he is. Whether it is Europe shaken by the French Revolution, or the deserts of Asia, or Walden Pond, the seer is the consummation and reality. His broomstick, if he travel astride of that, may range over deeps as dark as the gulfs in the Milky Way; and yet another kind of traveller may convert the region which holds the culture of the Chinese into a mere album of photographic snapshots and interlined facetiousness.

Seeing is of faith, for faith is not blind. There can be no faith without light. What we do not see may condemn us. What traveller would dare to interpret the world which he thinks he sees today? There is harder travelling now than kept Marco Polo so long from his home. There is no simple problem of a Grand Khan now. There is no Tartary. Cathay is a republic, complete with civil strife, Western ideas, and the machinery of industry. Communists interrupt the railway service of Java. Messer Marco Polo in all his wanderings saw nothing stranger than that, nor more difficult to read. Instead of Venice and Canton we have London and New York. A man flew to

Baghdad and back the other week in contemptuously few hours; and Persia weaves prayer-mats,
not to point to Mecca, but to help the sentiment
of English suburban villas. One may buy Burmese
gems by the pint by taking a penny bus from
Charing Cross; there is no need to voyage to
Cairo, Calicut, and Peking, to see the Orient. It
is mostly in the Cutler Street warehouse, by
Houndsditch. The Underground Railway serves
the Orient.

But we are not satisfied. A vague desperation
is suggested in our tours round the world. Something is missing from our civilization. Perhaps
we think that the farther we go the more likely
we are to recover whatever it is we have lost. It
is possible that the Communist risings in the Garden of the East come of the same disquiet which
sends rich Westerners circling the globe. Why
should the Hindus and Javanese revolt? Their
lives are more secure now than they were under
their old emperors and rajahs. And why should
rich men shut up their ancestral country seats and
go to the South Seas for the simplicity which began to die there as soon as Watt learned the way
to harness steam? The affliction appears to be
world wide. It is felt in Benares, Peking, and
Park Lane. The lions of Africa are being dis-

placed by sisal fibre, just as speedways and coal-mines are destroying Kentish orchards. We read that an imaginative explorer, instead of gratitude for his seclusion in a tropical forest, considered that the trees were growing to waste; they ought to be turned into wood-spirit. He was a modern traveller. He did not call the forest *Green Mansions*, nor see Rima there. He saw a potential reservoir of alcohol.

That may be our trouble. The faith may be dying which sees beauty in the world, and without knowing it that may be why we are desperate to escape from our toils. We are no longer able to wonder, even at our own ingenuity. We are not as little children, so the kingdom is lost. It is useless to voyage to Papeete to look for the kingdom. The Venetian noble, Nicolo de Conti, early in the fifteenth century, when his ship was in the Red Sea, was surprised to see elephants equipped for war; but he would have been still more surprised had he heard at night voices that were speaking in Venice; as I heard one night, off Cape Bon, the movements of dancers in a London hotel—through the sough of the dark, far at sea, I could hear London shuffling its feet; and that thought, if sufficiently examined afterwards when one was by the bulwarks alone, was enough

196

"... That burnt region of sand and rock
with its dangerous and rhapsodical
nomads...."

gan travelling and adventuring about 1425, reports for his day a Europe which in most respects is inexplicable to us. There was no New Learning then. When Tafur entered France, Joan of Arc had been dead only seven years. The English had been driven out of Paris, but were still in Rouen. The Mediterranean was still the centre of gravity of European commerce; not then had Portuguese navigators made the discoveries which would shift that commerce to the Atlantic seaboard, though, curiously enough, Tafur shows that one mart of Flanders was then richer than Venice, and the shipping of Sluys enormous in its tonnage. America was unknown. The Turks were encamped about Constantinople, where the Eastern Empire was about to fall. The Pope was an exile. The plague was in France, and that land was desolate with the wars of the fourteenth and early fifteenth centuries. We cannot, with those reminders, picture such a Europe. But in some chance ways, and without conscious design, Tafur does that for us. It is the wayside incidents of his story which betray a Europe we know quite well. He had been astonished by the riches of Bruges, and he went to Sluys to see the ships. At Mass there a woman approached him in secret, and wondering, he went home with her. There she offered him one of her two young daughters. The family was starving. All that commercial activity of Flanders and its wealth of luxuries, and this family had nothing to eat! How far, since Tafur's day, have our many inventions taken us? Have we got any distance, in our flying-machines?

Even while a doubt about our progress begins to disturb us, old habits compel the consideration of the conversion of beauty into still more starvation and smoke. We are not sufficiently afraid of troubling the stars by darkening the splendour of our planet; yet a doubt grows that what we think and do may not be inconsequential beyond the orbit of the earth. In that space beyond, where we cannot go, it is possible that some emanation from our liveliness finds its way, and not fortuitously. We may make a mark without knowing it. It is irrelevant to the story, no doubt, that one night at sea we chanced to hear revellers at Charing Cross, yet it was a warning not easily quieted. We have now learned beyond question that our various noises are indeed registered where we had supposed there was nothing but the impersonal sough of the dark.

There was a sometime Archdeacon of Westminster, Richard Hakluyt, who celebrated the earlier English seamen and travellers. His tablet in Bristol Cathedral reads: "His studious Imagination discovered new Paths for geographical Science and his patriotic Labours rescued from oblivion not a few of those who went down to the Sea in ships to be Harbingers of Empire, descrying new Lands, and finding larger Room for their Race."

That tablet is but just to Hakluyt. Yet consider its implications. The Westminster Archdeacon, without meaning to do it, who desired indeed to light an imperial desire in an adventurous people, did much to prompt the pall over the Black Country. His patriotic labours at length poured out as smoke from our factory chimneys; an odd outcome of a pure and selfless personal devotion. That dark sign of profit to an imperial people was the inevitable result of the valour and enterprise of Elizabethan seamen. Those harbingers of Empire and their celebrant, as now we see them, were moved in their age by an influence which stirred even its poets; they were compelled by a law of growth in a changing world, we may suppose, to which their community had to respond as though it had no more conscious control of its destiny than the annual flowers of the field. All these men together gave our country, gave the civilization we call West-

ern, a mighty shove towards the place where now
we find it. The glorious flower of the civilization
which romantically they predestined for us unfolded vast and strange at the end of a factory
chimney.

Thus so different may be man's pure intent
from its issue. Drake, returned from the shades,
we will imagine, with Hakluyt, to view what
substance we have given to the dreams they had
of other lands and seas, would have to agree with
the poet of their own day that there is a destiny
which shapes our ends whatever ardent measures
we take. Hakluyt, while contemplating, as a
shade, our motor-ships, our problem of credit,
our bickering over the size of the guns we shall
use against each other, and the difficulties involved, as in India, in that larger Room for the
Race, and the air route to Malacca, might recall
his visit, as a boy, a visit evidently so fruitful,
to his cousin, a Gentleman of the Middle Temple.
It was a trivial incident, that half-holiday visit,
to have had its casual part in shaping the problem
of the protection of British trade routes without
giving America a cause for war. For his cousin
but gave him a first lesson in geography. Young
Richard found lying in that chamber of the Mid-

dle Temple "certaine bookes of Cosmographie, with an universall Mappe."

There is no doubt the Westminster scholar was wakened by his cousin. The subject of geography was given, even on a holiday, quite a cheerful appearance; but the year of that lesson, we must remember, was little more than a decade after Sir Hugh Willoughby tried to reach Cathay and the Moluccas by the Siberian coast. From the map the Gentleman of the Middle Temple turned to the Bible, and directed the boy to read the 107th Psalm. Young Hakluyt did so, and his own contribution towards the industrial era and his country's imperial destiny was at once made certain.

"Which wordes of the Prophet together with my cousins discourse (things of rare and high delight to my young nature) tooke in me so deepe an impression, that I constantly resolved, if ever I were preferred to the University . . . I would by God's assistance prosecute that knowledge and kinde of literature, the doores whereof (after a sort) were so happily opened before me."

We are told that a civilization must grow to its height and then decline, like a flower of the field in its due season. Yet unlike the weed, a civilization passes through its predictable phases

to its sere, though to no harvest; it only dies; its
seed is potent for no future spring. The philosophers do not explain what lunar influence governs
its rhythmic rise and fall; they tell us largely but
of powers which bring a civilization to its height,
from which it shall lapse till only the barren
sands show where its hearths used to be warm,
and its priests to chant to its gods. It has its pioneers, its early explorers and prophets; then its
period when the profit-makers are assured of a
bounteous continuity through a special favour of
Providence, for they know they are more worthy
than the lesser breeds; and follow them its
patriots and celebrators, who praise the familiar
scene, now flushed in a serene autumn that is
everlasting, as they hope and believe. Will not
their assurance of their own worth hold in
perpetuity the splendour of the after-glow? No.
We see now there never was and cannot be an
empire on which the sun shall never set. All civili-
zations and empires must make their predestined
curves and fulfil their cycles.

Yet theories, though they seem flawless, should
not cause us to brood. No theory can be right
which satisfactorily encloses all that is known.
We do not know all. Little alien and unimportant
items are left out of the reckoning, forlornly

overlooked and unaccounted, yet presently to make the balance and fulfilment of a perfect formula as useless as a net when there are no fish. It is the way of a wilful mystery that its bottom is no sooner viewed than it falls out. Old night is still below.

It is true that the relative objective world may be almost anything a philosopher desires to name it, yet occasionally it does break into his subjectivity with an extrinsic brick, as it were, an interruption which causes him to surmise that something must have thrown it at him. We have been forced of late to develop theories explaining this age of machines, and to see omens of its impending doom. When our machines stop, so shall we. Civilized man, it appears, has passed out of the phase of imaginative exploration and experiment; he has created engines to do his work for him, but his soul has lost its daring, and he is now a subdued captive, chained to the wheels, a helpless slave in the mechanical establishment he created.

But maybe the urgency of this age of machines will slacken. Some Doughty may explore its polished and efficient desert, and his word may begin to rust it; its impulse will falter and its wheels slow down. Though man now can fly to explore the skies, he may cease to want to—anyhow, for the reasons which now lift him from the earth. After all, it is certain that in time man will see that the relentless cranks and wheels, for which he never had more than a boyish and fevered love, are only the thoughts of his youth. He got those wheels because he wanted them. Does he want them now? Presently we may pause to consider this devotion of ours in a temple which is a factory, where the dynamo is the presiding god, the ritual exacting and numbing, and engineers the priests. That would be natural in us. The theory of the rise and fall of a civilization may be able to stand all known tests as easily as a bright and perfect machine accurately revolving; but suppose we change our mind about it? The machine stops. The subservience of men to the despotism of the polished steel rods and the ordained revolutions of the wheels may weary. The boy may tire of his engine.

Mankind is not of the automatic stuff to worship any god beyond the period of the god's most severe exactions. In the long run men and women cease to do what gives them no fun. Over goes Dagon when he demands more than his worshippers care to give. He will be lucky if he gets much attention after he has compelled that crisis.

⟨All in a Night

It was whispered to me that the gaffer, who had just gone to sit over in that corner, was in his ninety-fifth year. He composed himself in a chair with decision and suppleness. That made me look again. I had seen the little old fellow enter, and he had come into the room down the three steps trippingly. His cheerful eye took us all in at once, as he nodded, and his skin was clear and pink. He began to attend to our talk, while sucking a clay pipe—the pipe was even an indecent antiquity—shyly, or slyly, but closely. The much younger men gave him little attention, but they were kind to granddad. Now and then they patronized him with a word or two, but direct sympathetic attention appeared to embarrass him. He might not have wanted our sympathy, but only his beer and a smoke.

A hydroplane had just passed over the house, from the sea. We were talking of flying. There had been a bad accident, and the evening paper, pink upon the table, was full of the explanations and reassurances of the experts. The gaffer was told about it, and he nodded with a show of bright understanding. We must expect accidents, we said, when doing what men had never done before. He smiled and approved. The man next to me grinned, and lowered his voice at my ear.

"He doesn't get it. The old un was in the Crimean War."

Why, that was in the youth of railways! Battleships then were the same as Nelson's, though some of them had an engine like a coffee-grinder. No Suez Canal. No telephones. Two months to get to India. I looked at the gaffer, not across a century, but across a change of mind. Time and space had altered. Something was said about a man who had flown to India, and back, in a few days. The gaffer twinkled and nodded. He knew. He had seen us flying.

And the great speed of these bird-men! That evening, traces remained with us of the ecstasy over the races for a Schneider Cup. "Dad," called out one of us across the table "did you notice the speed of one British flyer?" Dad took his pipe out of his mouth, and waited.

"Three hundred and thirty miles an hour!"

The young schoolmaster considered this. "Terrific," he said. "Let's see. Now that would get a man to the moon in about a month."

"Hear that, Dad? To the moon in a month."

The pipe was removed again hesitatingly. "The moon?" he quavered.

"That's right, the moon."

"What for?" the old man asked.

There were some chuckles. The idea was too much for him. "Well, that's how things go, Grandpa."

The gaffer's head nodded, or wobbled, but he smiled brightly. We disregarded him, while debating close estimates of the greater expedition with which work nowadays could be done. Now look here! Could you beat this? And when I started my job, one man demonstrated, and that's not so long ago, if I had to go to London, it was all day. All day. Wait for a train, then three hours, stopping everywhere of course, wait for a train again, everything messed up. Late at night. But only yesterday in my car I wiped it all up and was back home again early afternoon. The motorist made a helpless movement with his hands to express the indescribable difference we had advanced in the years since he started his job. You can go anywhere now, almost, breakfast in London, lunch in Paris, supper at home. Constantinople. Australia in a fortnight. What about it? We thought about it all, in an interval while some more full pots were being put on the table.

The refilling of the pots and some newcomers caused us to sort ourselves anew. I found myself next to the gaffer. He did not look at me, but grated his chair on the flags a little, to make room. The young barmaid, by invitation, contemptuously switched on the loudspeaker, and then the electric light as a vicious afterthought, and went so brusquely, in spite of a friendly arm to stay her, that she might have despised the lot of us. An instant metallic braying from above would have drowned the conversation but that our voices were raised to resist it. What was coming through? I was handed the *Radio Times*. A symphony was coming through, "Le printemps," by a new composer, from a concert of modern music in London. Spring was coming through, interpreted by the music of the day, and it was spring as we know it, April of the latest, though the flowers were all behind this year, a blare of northeasterly brass, interjectory flicks of cold mud, an earache of discordant blasts, an April symphony of squalls, hail, and unemployment . . .

"Switch off that bloody row!"

A man moved quickly. Silence fell. Our own voices began again, dropped to quiet speech. Some of this wireless music was funny, we suggested, but you could always switch it off. There was a man broadcasting the other night, and he said,

Bunk. Best I've heard. All rot. What, with only two valves? Don't you believe it. You're wrong. Get Berlin easy. Only cost seven and six. Heard it myself. Young Pepsy, he told me. You can't teach him anything about wireless. That kid, he picked up a man in New Zealand the other night. Heard him plain. Get out. New Zealand, I tell you. Heard every word he said.

The gaffer nudged me eagerly. "What did he say?"

"He heard a man speaking in New Zealand, Dad."

"Ah!" The gaffer fumbled back his pipe, but did not seem satisfied.

I was not quite sure about the old man's mono-syllable. A little baffled by his blue eyes, which blinked too intelligently for senility, I took a glance at him sideways. But he met my look with his own. His thin outstanding red ears, with pur-ple threads in them, seemed pricked up, as though alert. He held his pot on his knee. His boots were as rough and solid as lumps of grey rock. Maybe he had worn them as long as his feet. His brass watch chain was bought at a sheep-fair when Delhi was besieged, very likely. Yes, all very well to see him so, with his clothes hanging on him like an old drab skin he could no longer fill. His mouth was senile, or else his pipe made it weakly droop; but he had the eye of a bird ancient in all but its puckish stare, and his ears were pricked and on the alert. Was he a clod or did he once play on oaten pipes? A queer grin he had, for his age. He did not appear to mind my innocent filial condescension. I do not think he noticed it. He was an outworn labourer, content with what he was, and he had no envy.

His feet were far from three hundred and thirty miles an hour, going forward, but he could travel backward on a road a long distance in no time. He had that little advantage. He contemplated me aloofly, or else absent-mindedly, showing a yellow tusk, and for so long that I began to feel a little nervous; was I only just coming through to his cynical apprehension from the past? Hadn't he really noticed me substantially before? "He, he!" he snickered, "only to think of it. They do get about, so I've heard." He gave a semicircular flourish with his pewter pot, then brought it to his mouth in slow reverence. Perhaps none of the young men there had ever witnessed that ancient way with the pewter. He wiped his mouth with the back of his hand. "They do gad about." He shook with inward mirth. "Time was and they had six bathing-machines at this place; now they've got flying-boats, lots o' them. It do seem mazy." He was mirthful.

The cheerful indifference to us of this ancient made me suspect, most unreasonably, that perhaps life could be good, even when not assisted by appliances. It struck me that I might not have got that suggestion while watching a champion steering a craft roaring through mid-air like a comet, though such a transit is the nearest we have yet got to the Sun God with his chariot, if we except that minor competition of Shakespeare's. I tried to beguile from him some peeps into the past, and he was not unreluctant. It amused him. But they did not belong to us, those peeps, for they were mostly bucolic; there were fragments of a harvest-home of long ago, that hinted at bacchanalian joys. That gave my thoughts another turn. Had things improved, did he think, since his young days? "Yes, yes," he nodded. "Yes, yes, I suppose so, things be restless out of count. But I don't see we be any happier,"—he waved his pipe—"if you look 'ere, and you look there. Yes, they've improved." His mouth took a twist, but if he cackled I did not hear it.

Not any the happier for it? The queer old fellow, who certainly was happy in his own way, would be unable to understand what is plain enough to us; we do not look for happiness; we only wish to keep busy. He would not understand that impulse. It made the young men laugh, that chance question of his about a swift lunar trip. What for!

The loudspeaker was started again, and a firm voice began to advise us on the right way to cook potatoes. I left the tavern, and went along the quay to my lodgings, and began to read an account from the Dutch of a seventeenth-century voyage to the East. It translated me from that village of the English Channel into some distant seas which I knew slightly, and, while reading, the inconsequential notion came that I had met the gaffer before. The idea made me frown at it. What had he to do with this voyage? A stuffed fish in a case stared into futurity with a glass eye. There was a call in the dark without, from across the water, and the creaking of a ship's boom. Why should the gaffer reappear, as it were, in the midst of a Dutch navigator's yarn? Somehow I felt the old fellow was in accord. If I had met him before, where could it have been?

A chart in the book, which I was idly scanning, while thinking of another matter, gave me the clue. Pulo Kerchil was the place, though per-

haps not the same pulo mentioned by the seventeenth-century Dutchman. Somewhere about
there, though. There are many tiny islands in
those seas, and all are much alike. It was an old
fellow I had met out there, years ago. He had
pawky eyes. He had a local reputation as a *pawang*, a wizard. He could, as a *pawang* should
when he so desires, change his shape. You never
could be sure that he was not lurking near. He
was very old, I was told. He was alive during the
great earthquake—not the other earthquake,
forty years ago, when the village was shaken,
and some fishing boats were lost, but the great
one, when the sun went out, when the sea came
in, and many died. What year was that? Tuan,
who would know? It was the year of the great
earthquake.

That was near enough. I had gone then to the
Directions for Pilots in those seas, a book which
offers only ascertained facts, and I had learned
that the *pawang* must be one hundred and ten
years old. The *Directions* informed me that the
great earthquake was in 1813. No doubt then
about it. He must be a *pawang*.

I was on the island a week before I met him,
for though the island was small, it had no fa-
cilities for travellers. It was not easy to get away

217

from the village and the plantations. Behind us and around were swamps, and steep and wooded fastnesses, where reasonable men could have no business whatever. There were two tracks, and one ended by a ravine, apparently bottomless, on the side of a mountain, and another lost itself in a mangrove swamp. Nobody had shown an interest in Pulo Kerchil since a Dutchman landed there three centuries ago. For a week time stood still for me; it might have been a week of the year in which the Dutchman discovered Pulo Kerchil. Nothing had happened since, nothing to show the lapse of only a few centuries. The sky, the sea, the forest, the swamps, even the bamboo houses of the village and the fishing-boats and their men, could have been either in this age, or in that.

One afternoon, when the village was abandoned to the heat, and the beach to its sleeping palms, I found another track up the mountain. After climbing for an hour through the woods, I saw a slender bamboo with a white rag attached to it, like a pennant. That was odd—a taboo sign? A warning?

The track continued up. But was it a track, or a natural feature? There was not much light in the forest, and strange motionless shapes were

" . . . also, a man's own place was quiet"

posed about in the quiet. Sometimes, looking back and down, through a break in the trees, the sea was an illusion of sapphire, a lower sky. Yes, it was a track. It enlarged me presently into an area of full day, a cleared space with high foliage about it. There I rested, and watched one of the great bird-winged butterflies, a fellow in green and gold, making the only movement in a universe enchanted to an everlasting afternoon.

I was watching a butterfly. But something was watching me. How did I know? I didn't, but I could feel it. There was nothing alive in sight but the butterfly. At last there was no doubt about it, and I rose to descend, to leave that still open space. There behind me was an old Malay. How had he got so close without a sound? The brown mummy wore only a sarong, and his ribs and arms were skeletal. He was observing me in cheerful amusement, and for several reasons which instantly occurred I knew who he was. A nice place to meet a wizard.

I sat down again, and he squatted beside me. We did not speak, and I propitiated him with some tobacco. He examined the pouch closely, but said nothing. It was impossible not to be surprised that his shrivelled brown skin contained life as manifestly as bones, till I saw his beady

eyes watching me sideways, shyly, or slyly;
they were the same as the sunlight and the butterfly. They always had been there.

He pointed seawards, and spoke. We made
each other out with fair ease. He spoke simply,
slowly, and with gravity. He knew I was on the
island. He, from there, had seen my steamer depart. He was curious about that ship, the *kapal
api*, the fire ship; and the country from which
she had come, and the wonders of the world.

We knew, I told him, on that ship, that there
was trouble in Mecca between kings, and how
much was being paid in London for copra. Yet
how explain radiograms to him? Tuan, he said,
it is true we sometimes know what passes between
men, though they cannot see each other, and
nothing is said. Now I, Tuan, have often . . .

I nodded. I told him, too, that men now were
flying from the cities of the west to Java. They
came from far beyond Mecca. He considered
this. It was well known, he said at length, that
evil had wings, and could come through the air
in a day and a night. But, he added, happiness
was to be found in one place. Also, a man's own
place was quiet.

¶A Footnote to the War Books

As for this subject of the war, and especially of literature as it relates to the war, it is said that some of us are a little crazy. It would not be easy, and it is not necessary, to deny it. I was asked once—there was a kindly thought, perhaps, that if I tried I might still the importunities of a haunting shadow: "Why don't you write about it?" That idea I considered—it looked attractive —but while reflecting the bright hope it occurred to me that a cynical enemy could accuse me of having written about nothing else since 1914. He could make a sound case, too, I fear.

He could interrupt to show that evidence for a bat or two aloft is manifest in me at this moment. It is, but I do not repine. There is good company and confidential gossip in my favourite asylum. Some of us live there not only with the quick; there are also the ghosts, and they have nothing against us now. They are even cheerful and intimate. In our seclusion with ghosts and the bats we have something to gossip about which is not sex, though that occasionally intrudes; and is not politics, except in brief and comic asides; and is not the relativity of time and space and other human standards, because that notion is as familiar to us as home, and as the place-names of the Somme. But books we sometimes discuss, especially books on the subject which is our lunacy —and it is something, is it not, to be able to regard an object of art with an intimate knowledge of what it could portray?—because Heaven help the writer, who, we will instance, puts a tin hat on a soldier at Neuve Chapelle, or doesn't know the qualities of the various sorts of French mud.

Now we pass freely in and out of that dire eastern postern of Ypres known as the Menin Gate; it is comfortable to us at last. We recall, with a certainty of being understood, some other names, which are even deeper in time than Ypres: le Cateau, Soissons, Crépy-en-Valois, Meaux; for at least I heard the guns of the first battle of the Marne, without knowing at first whether they were to come this way or go that; but I heard those sounds grow less, for the first time in the early days of the war. No wild surmise upon a peak in Darien could have equalled my own, and that of two friends with me, in that bright September day. And for that and other reasons, which are no better than most that set cronies wasting time, I will confess that if now I get hold of a map of northwestern France I am lost for a spell.

A FOOTNOTE TO WAR BOOKS

I have been warned that this is indulgence. It is as deplorable in its effect, I am told, as bibbing.

What! To a fellow who heard men singing "Tipperary" in an autumn that seems to have been gone a century? To one who was frightened in the Ypres Salient when that appalling waste was already old, and tin hats and gas masks were all the go? When I stood amidst the dead on the Somme and the hills were erupting? Something to think about, there!

It cannot be helped now. Allow some of us to indulge—it is only more war casualties—and let happy and confident youth get on with its job of world reconstruction; for there, somehow, youth will kindly note, the ground still is, though cumbered with wreckage, for them to rebuild upon. And remember that there is this to be said for such an obsession as mine: though I saw something of it all, I was not a soldier. I but looked on, and therefore it happens to be my province to testify. Looking on was not altogether a task for a subsequent honourable decoration, I cheerfully admit, yet passively observing battle, and enduring long spells of the mud and monotony of war, was not so comfortable and interesting as might be supposed. It had its drawbacks. It is not so easy to watch other men do the dirty work; for one had to be with them, and sometimes when the occasion was distinctly unattractive. There was nothing—nothing worth speaking about—that one could do to help them. Most of them were youngsters, were even boys; and to have looked into their eyes, as one turned about for a quieter and safer place, and left to them a task they could not leave, is a haunting fact not easily exorcised. How can you and I dodge our responsibility for the work to which they had to be left in those days? For my part, I intend to rub it in till I die. It is about all I can do now. They left with us, we will bear in mind, their younger brothers, who mostly are unaware of the nature of war, even now.

But, you may reasonably plead, there have been other wars? That war was not peculiar, except in its extent and some details?

I can only reply that in the very early days of it, in August and September of 1914, you could have supposed the whole of Europe had been tilted up, and all its anciently established things were being up-ended and spilled down to the sea. It was a continental landslide. It was the greatest disturbance of mankind since the glaciers pushed out hunting forefathers down to the south. Was not that peculiar? The anciently established civil communities of Europe and their faiths were adrift again; and one may ask, Have they settled down yet?

We not only know they have not, but that they will not have settled down in our time. It has been said, I think by General Botha: "Humanity has struck its tents again, and once more is on the march." Whither?

So it begins to look as though we had about us something like a subject for an epic, if we could find the man to write it. And if it affords complaining critics any comfort, let them courageously pretend that what happened in Flanders and by the Marne and elsewhere was episodic; that such things have happened before, and may happen again. Let them pretend that they may pass over so many place-names in France, from Nancy to Dunkirk, names still portentous to some of us, as mere ploughlands once more, waste ground, cemeteries, and reconstruction. That will not do. It is useless to pretend, to deny, to ignore. I do not doubt that the men to whom Mons and Verdun and the Somme mean so much, were present when old Europe fell. They were right underneath when the roof came down. The downfall of Europe's august but faulty establishment, the end of the industrial era as our fathers knew it, with the collapse of its Imperialism under the weight of its own necessary and inevitable guns, and even rifts in its cathedrals and athenæums, are more than phrases. They really indicate inherencies of the common disaster and revolution. To the men who were in France they never were mere phrases. Those fellows read those phrases in a spectacle terrible enough to break up familiar acceptances and to destroy ancient faiths. The lesson could not have been more emphasized by a veritable archangel descending to earth to announce doom. There were days and nights on the Somme when the scene of earth suggested the day after the Last Day. "Things," the men used to say, "can't ever be the same again." They cannot be.

For some years after the war was over, publishers and readers were very shy of war books. Now, we learn, there is a distinct and growing disposition to revisit the glimpses. It is said that the public is now showing a desire to read, sometimes with wide approval, stories of war; stories of what we will agree to call The War.

The reading public was bound to come to that mood at last. During the conflict the emotions of the public were kept at high tension with shocks of propaganda, with rhetorical appeals to its love

of virtue, which was itself, and to its hatred of
vice, which was the enemy; with noble but brazen
music; with luscious stories of heroes. The end
came; and then it felt as did the man the morning after the orgy. Many good folk, too, who had
not been unaware of the falsities about them but
who sat patiently for years under bombing raids,
or had waited, hoping they would not get the
fatal message from the battle line which indeed
did at last come to them, tried to forget it, though
they found they could not. But they would not
speak of it and would not read any more about
it. Yet somehow, vaguely, they felt those years
of the war to be gravely significant. They
surmised fearfully that their fellow creatures
were the most dangerous animals on earth; were
likely, in fact, to wreck this planet in a mood of
resolute and exultant virtue. They lost faith in
their neighbours, a loss which is called by some
observers a revolt against democratic institutions;
they began to think that evil was stronger than
the healing powers, and to see progress only as
another name for change, generally for the worse.
They began to dread the impermanence of deli-
cate truth in this world of huge and arrogant lies.
They supposed, in fact, that most people worshipped a god who may be called Dagon, and that

attaining to peace and security. There is a possibility, we wonder, that good will may be safer than guns? We are losing an old dreary fatalism over whatever our governors, hidden behind an indifferent and cheerful public, may prepare for us, and are beginning to protest, with noticeable dislike, about being dragged into another obscene crime against intelligence like the last world-war. We know that the pomp and majesty of it, the sombre and throaty calls to national honour and great traditions, as now we give a backward glance, is all as ugly and distressing as foul play and a betrayal of the light. We are beginning to understand. That fine fellow we hear so much about, but never meet, the great military expert, who knows how to produce for us a security which the First Cause unfortunately omitted from the plans for genesis, if ever a final statue is raised to his memory will be shown with ears so long that happy wayfarers will never forget to laugh as they pass it. We are beginning to feel, in fact, that we may save our earth, if we try, and so are reading with a new interest, and for our better knowledge, what of truth there is to be got about the last affair.

How are we to recognise that shy virtue when we see it in a book? That recognition is not always an easy matter; yet is not the test for all literature the same? It is unimportant whether the subject is a nightingale in full song or the Passchendael ridges in 1917; we are, for some reason, aware of an unusual revelation. There is, we will say, unexpected light. There is no noise about light, and it is still. We are aware of what had been hidden from us. And light does not argue; it does not attempt to persuade; it is not rhetorical nor heroic. Like the common flowers of the field, which could well compare with the glories of a great king, light simply is. You need know nothing of the nature of light to understand well enough that you see things better by its aid than by, we will say, fireworks, which are so much more colourful, sensational, and decorative. Let us take, for one proof, a famous statesman's *History of the War*. The Rt. Hon. Winston Churchill's history has been welcomed, even by important critics, as "great prose." We should know something of prose, for we are not unaware of Browne, Bunyan, Swift, Sterne, and Lamb. There are also Melville, Hardy, and Doughty. So there is not much excuse for us when deliberately, after a critical scrutiny, which suggests we have a right to judge, we give to limelight the honour which should go to the broadening of

"... and see an outer world of dubious reflections and ominous shapes"

dawn. I have read the right honourable gentleman's recent and famous history, and I find this in its first volume. He describes for us the methods of diplomatists, and the consequence of their expert deliberations:

"They sound so very cautious and correct, these deadly words. Soft quiet voices purring, courteous, grave, exactly measured phrases in large peaceful rooms. But with less warning cannons had opened fire and nations had been struck down by this same Germany. So now the Admiralty wireless whispers through the ether to the tall masts of ships, and captains pace their decks absorbed in thought. It is nothing. It is less than nothing. It is too foolish, too fantastic, to be thought of in the twentieth century. Or is it fire and murder leaping out of the darkness at our throats, torpedoes ripping the bellies of half-awakened ships, a sunrise on a vanished naval supremacy, and an island well-guarded hitherto, and at last defenceless?" "We may picture it," this writer assures us, "this great fleet, with its flotillas and cruisers, steaming slowly out of Portland Harbour, squadron by squadron, scores of gigantic castles of steel wending their way across the misty shining sea, like giants bowed in anxious thought."

Steel castles bowed in anxious thought! Wireless whispers! Belly-ripping torpedoes! Murder leaping out of darkness! It gives a reader the fear that the performer may, in his exultation, step right over the footlights and let his eloquence have its way on the big drum.

Is wisdom there? It looks to me as though there were a lack of control, which is not wise. Is light there? Yes, of a kind, the kind which comes in chromatic beams from the wings to give an object on the stage an appearance it does not own. It is, I should say, eloquence in an Eton collar on Speech Day. It is intended to impress us; and we may doubt that genuine eloquence ever so intends. "But the iniquity of oblivion blindly scattereth her poppy, and deals with the memory of men without distinction to merit of perpetuity." That moves us; yet I think Browne was merely talking aloud to himself, a lonely man who was deeply stirred by his vision of the world, and felt the need to speak, yet had but one hearer. It was the expression of the natural rhythm of his mind. He was unconscious of it. If we think we ought to be eloquent because the subject deserves it, and try to be, then we are not. The test for a book about the war is the same as that for any other sort of book.

There is another war book which shows whether or not the quality of the writing is different where a writer is moved, first of all, by sympathy for his fellows and sorrow for their state. This passage, from C. E. Montague's *Disenchantment*, concerns Cologne, 1918, when the war was over:

"For the day of the fighting-man, him and his chivalric hobbies, was over. The guns had hardly ceased to fire before from the rear, from the bases, from London, there came flooding up the braves who for all those four years had been squealing threats and abuse, some of them begging off service in arms on the plea that squealing was indispensable national work. We had not been long in Cologne when there arrived in hot haste a young pressman from London, one of the first of a swarm. He looked a fine strong man. He seemed to be one of the male vestals who have it for their trade to feed the eternal flame of hatred between nations, instead of clearing out stables, or doing other work fit for a male. His train had fortunately brought him up just in time for luncheon. This he ate and drank with good will, complaining only of the wine, which seemed to me to be good, that it was not better. He then slept on his bed until tea-time. Reanimated with tea, he said, genially, 'Well, I must be getting on with my mission of hate,' and retired to his rooms to write a vivacious account of the wealth and luxury of Cologne, the guzzling in all cafés and restaurants, the fair round bellies of the working-classes, the sleek and rosy children of the poor. I read it, two days after, in his paper. Our men who had helped to fight Germany down were going short of food at the time, through feeding the children in houses where they were billeted."

That has no eloquence, except so much as indignation will give to good sense and kindly feeling when recording an outrage on fellowship. Montague gave us the first book on the war which compelled us to look upon that affair objectively, to see it as something which had a nature and history not necessarily related to the emotions we had cherished for more than four years. When his *Disenchantment* came for appraisement to the office where I posed as literary editor, I put it in my pocket, and for some reason got into an underground train and overshot several stations beyond my destination. I thought, indeed, I heard at last the accents of the truth about a matter, concerning which I knew, to my grief, Truth so far had said no more than she could get up from the bottom of her well when the cover was kept on it. If I chose to be critical, I might say that to be disenchanted one first must be enchanted. No matter; Montague, though much too old for it, did more than the fiercest fire-eater on the home front could have expected of a man of his years; he served in the line, and he served at a base when he was far too sagacious about battle and its relevant matters to be among Brass Hats. He had had to judge the flight of minenwerfers so that he might not be there when they burst; yet he also went to live in France at General Headquarters where he could watch such intrigues, described for us in that revealing story—not in the least fanciful, I have reason to know—*Honours Easy*, in his *Fiery Particles*.

There is no answer to his indictment. There you have the transit of a loyal soldier who happened to have a mind of his own, from his original pure intent in a high cause to the day when he had no illusions left. His book has been called sad. For that matter, we know that to read any masterpiece of literature exalts us with the suggestion of kinship with a noble line; and the shadow falls across its pages from the weird which man must dree. In my experience it is always there. And on the pages of *Disenchantment* the shadow is plain enough. What else would we

239

expect from that title, in the book of a sober comrade who would have us remember the nameless boy, seen by the light of a star-shell briefly in the desolation his betters had made, and then lost forever? We may be sure it was the strain of those years which ended Montague too soon. But his book remains, the first, and one of the best essays at recording those years we have had, or are likely to have. His book will endure. He would be the last to complain that he had to pay the full price for it.

There have not been enough books to go with it, even now, to make a lengthy bibliography. One of the earliest of the English—it is forgotten now—was called *Field Ambulance Sketches*, by A. Corporal. Let it be not thought unliterary to speak heartily of a corporal's sketches of ambulance work because Homer sang of Troy. What is Troy, when we remember Delville Wood? This corporal was at Neuve-Église, which is, or was, behind Plug Street, when the Germans broke through in April, 1918. The Corporal's was actually the first book I read of the front which was not heroic swipes. "Occasionally," he says, "above the darker gloom of the trees one of the new star-shells would rear its white face, like a cobra in an opium dream, and stand there a few moments, expanding its hood and slavering sparks, until, its suspicions apparently allayed, it faltered, relaxed its watchful pose, and sank again to cover." When a man can write like that about a star-shell he is worth attention when he has to tell us of Passchendael in 1917. He was there with a group of stretcher-bearers, playing cards in a dug-out, waiting for "zero," which was 3.30 A.M.; and later there was a man on a stretcher, with no face, who had a last message to give them; and the man wished to confess that, just before the grenade got him, he had stolen a pot of marmalade. He was grieved, that man. He wished to own up before he died.

That pot of marmalade is more momentous than a Cabinet Minister's steel castles bowed in anxious thought. For the truth is simple. It is of the heart; the mind will give it form, but had better not attempt to improve it. From the desire to heighten and improve came the books about the war which we will not read now, though once we thought they were wonderful. The impulse to suggest the sound of drum-fire by words resembling the rolling of drums is dangerous. The sound of drum-fire was hardly that, except superficially. What was that stately sound? Perhaps it was no more than beat through the mind of the

draper's assistant when he heard it, and knew
he must make his way stoutly right into it,
through the mud and wire. Perhaps if we want
Truth at any time we shall have to surprise
her. She is shy. Words rolling like drum-fire
seem to scare her clean out of sight. Her secret
is in the heart of the draper's assistant, and he,
poor fellow, doesn't know it. After all, though
with klaxons, loud speakers, and other mechanical aids for making presences known, it still may
not be in the wind and not in the tempest that
Truth is speaking; yet we are in such a hurry
nowadays, and are on the alert for such stentorian
warning of what is important, that we may completely miss hearing that fabulous gentle voice.
And better for our composure, perhaps, that we
are deaf to it; for when and if it is heard, it
will make a difference. As simple and inevitable
as the Parables, I remember, were Georges Duhamel's short stories of the war. You will find
them in two books, *Civilization* and the *New
Life of Martyrs*. When you begin one of his
stories about a prone figure in a casualty station—
Duhamel was a surgeon, but he is also a poet—
you are at once arrested. You are not too pleased
about it, either, if you do not wish to change your
preconceptions of heroes. But that French sur-

geon's eye is compelling, though mild. It does
not permit an easy escape. And presently, with
oblique and trifling words that suggest a more
dreadful doom than that brought to a ship and
her men by the untimely death of an albatross,
you find your notion of the war suffering a
change. The Irish have a saying that a man may
sleep comfortably on another man's wound. And
Duhamel tells us that man must suffer in his
flesh alone, and that that is why war is possible.
Then he tells us a story or two.

Yes, he has disclosed the secret. We can so
easily bear the sufferings of others, especially if
we do not even hear the boy crying in No Man's
Land where none may aid him. Let us imagine
that in a war every civilian concerned developed
continuous neuralgia, which could ease and van-
ish only when "Cease fire" sounded on the battle
front. Now think of the long queues of people,
their sallow faces wrapped in flannel, to be seen,
dismal and grievous, waiting for an urgent word
with premier or president, waiting to consult noble lords and senators and right honourable gen-
tlemen on the period set for their agony; and
those august experts, poor noble fellows, helped
by fire in all their teeth, would themselves be
wondering in involuntary tears whether it were

better to use common sense, or go on to a knock-out blow, bankruptcy, and still larger cemeteries of heroes. But man suffers in his flesh alone; and that is why war is possible. Yet Duhamel does in a measure resolve the cruel enigma. One cannot read his stories without finding that pity and remorse diminish the glorious and ecstatic show of war, and silence its trumpets and drums with the sight of a man in a bed, who, in a sense, is now no man at all. His decoration lies on the coverlet, but he does not see it. The war is what went on in the mind of the draper's assistant, and of his wife, who, one evening, stood with an official telegram at her gate, and stared down the empty road.

Out of sheer gratitude for a novel which reads like that of a master, free, cheerful, and even exuberant, critics have hailed *Sergeant Grischa* as the first really great novel of the war. That is not right. R. H. Mottram's *Spanish Farm* trilogy is just as masterly in its scope and significance, and it happens to be English. Mottram's rendering of the scene in Flanders is a gift of the gods, and we ought to be proportionately grateful for receiving what we never get except the gods are kind to us. The *Spanish Farm* entitles the English to speak up for themselves in this matter of war literature. Nevertheless, you cannot read the opening chapters of *Sergeant Grischa* without recognizing in surprise and wonder the signs of genius at its task, absorbed and happy, haughty in its sweeping gestures, careless of our habits of thought, bringing things to pass out of what seems to be nothing, showing us casual irrelevances which grow into significance as we look on in bewilderment. There the rare miracle is. Germany in that book is shown to be what any nation must be in war, when logic shall justify all crimes beneficial to a noble cause, when lies undergo a change and become truth, and deceit is a virtue, and the worst is the best. War makes every pushful duffer important. It cheers all the eager busybodies. It liberates to full usefulness, for our improvement, every humbug, coward, and charlatan, who sees his opportunity. The good men mostly die; the others live on. Sergeant Grischa dies.

There is Edmund Blunden's *Undertones of War*. Something in Blunden's story is more than queer. As you read deeply into it your uneasiness grows. This poet's eye is not in a fine frenzy rolling. There is a steely glitter in it. It appears to be amused by drolleries not obvious to us. It is as though, in the midst of a pleasing and animated

conversation after dinner, you fancied you heard
distant and indeterminate music not altogether
unfamiliar. What was that? You withdraw your
attention a little from the talk to get a clue to
those disturbing strains; you become absent in
mind from the lamplight and the cosy talk, and
see an outer world of dubious reflections and
ominous shapes, a region vast and dark and as
cold to human hope and aspiration as a polar solitude. What, at dinner? Yes, there the heads of
happy talkers remain between you and that fore-
boding night, still animated and unaware, and
they continue to say nothing while making foolishly eager movements. You have to pull yourself together—come out of that disturbing dream
—begin to chatter again with the others. Blunden's book, in fact, is by a ghost for other ghosts;
some readers will not know what it is all about;
they will say so, not being ghosts, and seeing none.
Yet it is a humorous book, though its fun is wan;
through its pale fun you can see the tangibilities
of today solid in their appropriate places. You
soon have more than a suspicion that Blunden is
not addressing us at all, but presences not visible.
His cheerful voice is addressed over our shoulder,
and our amusement fades when that fancy chills
it. We turn round, and nothing is there! This

ghostly play, once we are aware of it, disturbs our confidence in the tangibilities of our own hearty day with a hint that there are tidings withheld. What is it the shades know and laugh over?

Blunden says nothing about that. Why should he? The shades would know it, and so need not be told. Yet the uneasy reader persists in trying to find out. He suspects that this is a rare book in which much is secreted in the blank spaces; the best of it, maybe. He might be overhearing, by chance, allusive but exciting reminiscences by men out of sight. At first he supposes their shattering adventures were by the body and of the sword; then becomes awed by more than a suspicion that these reminiscences are of something worse than the blood, mire, and the shocks of war's explosions. Somebody was shot through the heart, we gather, yet continued to smoke and laugh. Something was worse than the fury of the enemy. What was it? The listener wonders whether it might have been the old folk at home; for the soldier appears to have been lonelier in spirit when in London and more antagonistic to what was current there than when on his belly at night behind the German wire wondering whether he would get what was meant for him. He had a better understanding of Fritz than of us. We were the aliens. There was understanding through common adversity in France; in London there was but a revival of the old horrible hue-and-cry, and to the soldier home "on leave" that was dismaying. Yet no. It is not that. Though that may have been so, it will not account for all we find in Blunden's book—or rather, for what falls across it like a shadow, sounds through it as an elfish laugh. Is it any good trying to understand the ghost of a child who has played knuckle-bones in hell for shocking forfeits? As a haunting presence it has some upsetting ways, especially when it would play with us by the study fire, after midnight. You find yourself hoping that nobody else in the house heard that laugh. Somehow, though, its spectral merriment is more to us than all the starry host.

There is loveliness in this narrative of Blunden's. Let no man read it who fears the magic of names: Mesnil, Beaumont Hamel, Givenchy, Festubert, Mazingarbe, Zillebeke, Thiépval, Richebourg St. Vaast. And Ypres! The jags of that city's pallid ruin, with imprisoned echoes jibbering at the hurrying wayfarer, rise again in Blunden's story. The fellows who went through the Menin Gate of Ypres and vanished, they live again, and glints and suggestions of the

night which swallowed them; the face of a pal
seen for a moment by the light of a star-shell;
the friends in a dug-out eyeing each other while
waiting to be buried ("we do not exist"); the
elder chum who ignored the worst of it, whose
complexion was always rosy, whose solidity could
not be moved by any sudden frightfulness, and
who jollied his weaker brethren then with
steadying advice; the boozy sergeant-major,
good-humoured and soft, who became a centre of
gravity when things went wrong. After all, the
men are the best of Blunden's book; and that is
right. That at least we were sure to get from a
poet. This story of war stirs and proceeds with
living figures, and its scenes are authentic with
trifles forgotten till Blunden reminds us of them.
The old front line comes back. It is solid. You
can hear the mud of The Salient when the duck-
boards squelch under the feet of unseen men
"going up" at night. You can smell the Somme.
You may potter around Mesnil, and shudder
again in the silence of its ghastly sunlight. And
if to stir those apprehensions does not mean we
are reading good prose, then there is no other
way of proving it that I know. Yet there is more
in the book than that. Something æolian breathes
through its lines. You may hear echoing, as one

without Siegfried Sassoon's war poems. They have grown essential to it, like the familiar and allusive voice of a friend who knows, without prompting, where one's thoughts are at midnight. Through Sassoon's poems sound the intimacies of men whose voices we shall never hear again.

And the other poets—and we ought to pay some attention to their common opinion—tell us of a young soldier, who went west just before the final signal was given, and who left with us a poem called *Strange Meeting*. You will find it in a slim volume published by Chatto & Windus. Owen's fellow poets tell us, in confidence, that *Strange Meeting* is the best poem out of the war. And I think we may, when reading it a second and a third time, begin to hear then, in strange music, a lament for all that light and loveliness which was extinguished too soon, when we were so very sure our ardours and endurances were establishing the right of virtue to exist upon the earth. The man was slain who wrote *Strange Meeting*. He died within reach of the Armistice. And so now, as the echoes die away from our late victorious cheering, we may, by chance, if reflective in the ensuing quiet, hear the faint echo of another appealing cry of long ago . . . "For they know not what they do."

Yet it is said that heroes are the less heroic when they cry out, though in a measure which makes poets of them, against the hardships and suffering inevitable in war. It is a sign in them, some people say, of softness. They may be poets then, but are less than stout men. The true soldier endures the worst we can inflict upon him and says no word. We are told to believe that only inferior men cry out when they are hurt; it may be taken as sad evidence that civilization weakens character when young soldiers, having survived the mud and explosions of four years of warfare, emerge from their hell to tell us what it was like, and to protest against so cruel an iniquity.

It may be so. Yet we ought to remember that it was a point of honour in Red Indians to keep a straight face even when they were being flayed alive. Savage men endure afflictions stoically, even to death, without any quickening of the intelligence. They never reflect that their punishment may be the consequence of savagery. We hear of an appeal to Heaven forced out long ago by torture, when the victim felt he was forsaken. Was that a sign of a soft defect in the character of the victim?

My own surmise is that this stern reproval of

252

protesting young soldiers by cool and realistic critics is in itself a sign of secret fear. When people are afraid, they greatly dislike having the cause of their fear indicated to them. They will not look at it, and get angry when invited to do so. They assert roundly that they are superior to whatever may be disturbing their minds. Good men, it was my experience when watching men at war, fear not to confess their fear, for they are aware that the stoutest heart never knows when it may fail. This reproval of anguished cries forced from torn bodies and lacerated minds by the cruelty of the machine-made horror of modern war is itself merely a sign of timid barbarism. Barbarians keep straight faces under torture; that is the barbaric code. We hear that Priam forbade the Trojans to weep when, during a truce, they and the Greeks were burying their dead. He thought weeping would soften his men, and that they would show less resolution on the morrow. Agamemnon did not ban sorrow to the Greeks; he was not afraid of his men. A soft-hearted man I know, a gunner, during one of the final ferocious battles in France, had a brother in the line before his guns. The infantry that day captured the German trenches; they broke the Hindenburg line. And that gunner, advancing his

ℂOne January Morning

It was January 12, 1928, and its dawn gave my empty suburban street an unrecognizable look of splendour. I think the chimneys of our houses were of gold, and the walls and roofs of jasper and amethyst, which is nothing like them. That glowing and unfamiliar vista was as if I had surprised a secret celebration of the earth and sky; we were not supposed to see it; it was to fade into our own place before we were about. As I looked out on my changed street I was repeating the haunting thought of the night, "Hardy is dead." But the thought, which astonished me, that I should see him no more, was in accord with the colours of that high dawn. We have so often remembered Hardy, because of an aspect of the earth and sky. The heavens and the earth were always the chief characters in the dramas of that poet; over mere mortals presided the eternal sky and the shadowy presences of the Norns. So it seemed right for the street to be empty, and to be strange with a transfiguring glow. Hardy had gone.

Within an hour, as the sunrise foretold, came the wind and rain. Roofs and sky turned to lead. The spurts of rain thickened the glass of my win-

255

dow. There was going to be time enough indoors
to think about Hardy, yet to think to little purpose; not really to think, but to stare unseeing
at the sullen clouds and the rain, for beyond them
was a dream world more vivid and stable than
the elements, a visionary country in which one
had strayed in the reading of nearly forty years,
and there had watched Destiny compelling men
and women who were better known than one's
neighbours—even though one cheerfully sus-
pected Destiny to be often a little too conscious of
its cheerless task to be veritable; and to remember
the venerable little man, whose magic had established that sublimation of the substantial but
changing world, as we saw him at Max Gate
shortly before his fatal illness began, sitting with
the brightness of a log-fire reflecting in his quick
eyes, while he talked blithely of poetry, specu-
lated on the prehistoric earthworks to be seen
from his house, and smiled at the gossip of the
town.

But though there was all day to think about
him, there was no likelihood of making a contribution to wisdom, no chance of a critical ad-
justment which would help to place the poet's
urn with precision. It was not the time to be dis-
passionate. And when we cannot stand apart from

our personal feelings we cannot be critics, for in criticism, as we know, we ought to do what it is so very difficult to do; we ought to consider the work of a poet apart from changeable human opinions, and see it simply as a timeless and isolated achievement bereaved of kinship. Luckily for Hardy's contemporaries, they are not called upon to be critics who will be strictly just to him by those fundamental laws of art which yet somehow include, when we so desire, any curious departure from tradition. It is not for us to attempt to use the impartial scales, but only to exalt him or otherwise, to explain his sublimity, or his want of taste, as the moods vary, and to declare whether this thing of his, or that, is consonant or not with the way we ourselves would have handled the matter, had his gift been ours; though certainly, as to one failing of the poet, most of us will agree. We cannot but observe, and with deep regret, Hardy's brooding sorrow over the ways of humanity. We have to question that perversity. How could so great a mind, in the face of our handsome progress, declare the unhappiness of our state? But we will not pause now to prove the poet's life-long error by pointing to those agreeable steps heavenward, in the late history of humanity, which joyfully mock the sad and compassionate poet; so compassionate, indeed, that he could not blame us when evil came of folly, but some Blind Will.

Today we must have differing views of Hardy, but it cannot be helped. Instinctively we shall separate, for we know what we want, the beauty of his work, which we desire, from the truth in it, which not seldom is undesirable. Hardy cannot succeed where Jesus failed. That truth and beauty seem strangely one need not concern those who prefer the simple method of separating what is comforting in a book from what is challenging and disturbing. We find it difficult to admit that a poet's thought may be beautiful because of its contrast with the darkness of our customary ways, for that would mean that beauty convicted us. It is not in the province of poetry to do that; it fails us when it is not an irrelevant solace at leisure, pleasant, as is wine, after the dustiness of a harsh and insistent world. We are not consoled when the god made in our image is charged with betraying our ugliness. So it need not surprise us that one of our most paradoxical and confident essayists, to whom good and evil are not ambiguities, but are easily defined and separated because his Church provides him with an infallible test, when his opinion was sought by

"... as if a dawn out of its appointed
order in the years had surprised
the place we know"

an interviewer on the news of the death of the
poet, said of the author of *The Dynasts* that
Hardy was a "nice courteous gentleman, rather
simple-minded." That is right, too, as far as it
goes, and indeed shows less intolerance than the
dismissal of Hardy merely as the village atheist
blaspheming over the village idiot. The essayist's
commendation is also applicable to so many people, fortunately, that it seems hardly worth space
in a newspaper to record virtues so usual. Then
again, the London daily papers, by their various
placards on the morning after Thomas Hardy's
death, betrayed the fact that not every one of
them was prepared on the instant to estimate the
importance of the news. Some of them did not
consider his passing to be more important than
some other subjects, which surprise compelled us
to note. One paper was anxious that we should
Read Our New Serial, "Frail Wives." Another
asked "Who will give Jix £100,000?" The con-
tents bill of another famous London daily paper
bore simply the cryptic numerals 1857428;
though whether those figures referred to a successful feat of circulation, or were indeed a caba-
listic advertisement of a fatal conjunction of
numbers which made inevitable the passing of a
great man, it was impossible for a non-reader to

guess. Yet another of our daily papers placarded an outburst entitled Ambassadors Cars. That may have been a special edition devoted to automobiles of luxury, but I cannot say, for I did not buy the paper. And later in the day one afternoon paper of the capital of the British Empire, a paper once famous for its liberal outlook on the world, gave a few grudging sentences to the news that the greatest figure in European literature, who happened to be English, had died, apparently because its editorial staff was too astonished by Mrs. Snyder's New Lease of Life. There were other periodicals, however, which did make the appropriate comment and whose estimates of the significance of the principal news of the day were serious; yet these little things show us that the stress of the exciting nature of the living day, is fears, dogfights, rumours, executions, crime, and market prices, tend to confuse our sense of values. It is not easy to turn from the attraction of what draws our attention to the estimate of the worth of a creator of beauty. Beauty, if it be there, will last longer than the interesting things about us, but that does not mean much to those who cannot see it. Said a London Councillor once, in the peroration of his speech which demanded the destruction of London's finest bridge, "as for its beauty, that the man who wrote *The Woodlanders* and *The Return of the Native* seemed not so clever as they. A meeting with Hardy was comforting to self-esteem. He was venerable, he was indeed already a legend; his great epic which placed him next to Shakespeare was published over twenty years ago; yet all that seemed rather odd, too, because the little old man himself, as he entertained us, might have been the youngest and most innocent of us all. He appeared content to talk of the habits of owls, and of the signs of the weather, of local inns and queer characters, and of the strangeness of hearing in Dorchester by wireless telephony the dancers' feet when an orchestra was playing at a London festival. Trivial life interested him. Little things amused him. Little things, you could see, often had for him a significance which a clever listener failed to grasp. Hardy was a simple man. A meeting with Hardy made it possible to understand why those very clever men about Shakespeare left for us such scant testimony of the fellow who wrote *Antony and Cleopatra*. That fellow of the Sonnets was a smiling and good-natured man, we must suppose, who was so simple there was little to say about him. He never made unkind epigrams, it was not easy to quarrel with him, and he did not get excited, not even when the Armada was scattered. Now and then, perhaps, he would drop a rare remark from his corner of the tavern, which made listeners stare, and wonder what he meant. There seemed nothing but queerness in it, until later, when the phrase was remembered because of an awkward coincidence in life. Then it became explicable, in a new light. Mere chance, though, that thought of his. It was the experience which brought the light. Shakespeare had spoken more wisely than he knew.

Hardy, too, had so innocent a guess into people and their motives that sometimes when talking to him you felt this child was as old as humanity and knew all about us, but that he did not attach importance to his knowledge because he did not know he had it. Just by chance, in the drift of the talk, there would be a word by Hardy, not only wide of the mark, but apparently not directed to it. Why did he say it? On the way home, or some weeks later, his comment would be recalled, and with the revealing light on it.

Max Gate is a walled little island of trees on the road to Egdon Heath, just outside Dorchester. No house can be seen from the road. I fancy Hardy planted most of that screen of leaves. It suggests the hiding-place of a recluse. There is an approach across the fields from the town, and in summer that was the way to go, with Came Hill lifting darkly beyond a sea of corn, and the isolated promontory sculptured by men long before the Romans landed, now called Maiden Castle, in the distance. The square tower of Fordington Church and the chimneys of the town floated near on the tree-tops of a hollow. You felt sure you would find Hardy in that country, even though the footpath was uncertain. It looked like his country. But it had fallen dusk in sharp winter weather when we were there last. In fact, it was the month before he died. The house then was only a lantern in a dim porch. A spray of cotoneaster had left the mass of shadow to get into the light of the lantern; it was the only sign of a wall.

Mrs. Hardy always knew how to keep out intrusions such as easterly winds. Her house was as warm and comforting that evening as a quiet heart. The old man, brisk and youthful, showed us where we should sit to get the benefit of the fire. There was a lazy smoke-coloured Persian cat, appropriately named Cobweb, who stretched and yawned, and was an assurance of the ease and rightness of the time and place. It was certainly the fireside to get to the heart of the matter, though leisurely. If our talk gave out, then there were the reflections of the lively fire playing on the face of the old poet, who contemplated the bright logs, his eyebrows raised, his legs stretched out, his hands between his knees. That seamed face lost sight of the visitors for a while, and its nervous interest in the gossip changed to the compassionate look of a man who had brooded for long on the world, but was not sure he had made out what it all meant, or could do it the good he desired for it. It may be true that as a man thinks so is he, and that may be why Hardy's head was satisfying with expected beauty. Some who met him say that you would not have known Hardy for a poet. Perhaps that is because the younger poets frequent the town, and are so often seen and heard. We get to think that a poet should resemble the pattern of a poet. Hardy did not. He resembled in no particular way any other poet you may have met. He might have been a retired solicitor of the country town, pursuing keenly in his leisure several hobbies, finding cheerful entertainment in the fact that his house was on the side of a patrician graveyard of the Romans, and that when gardening he sometimes turned up relics; that there were signs near by that men unknown had a grove to their god long

before Cæsar came; startling you with the remark
that Robert Louis Stevenson, when he saw him
last, was sitting in your chair; admitting
strangely then, for a man of his years, that he
read poetry nowadays and very little prose, but
that he enjoyed the prose of Sir Thomas Browne
and Lamb, and preferred Sterne to Swift. It
would not be odd, but quite in keeping, that a
retired solicitor should have a shrewder knowledge of men and women than a fashionable
novelist. His interests turned quickly with any
change of the conversation. He would give you a
rum story of a dog, and you had to admit it was
stranger than your own anecdote; so very strange,
indeed, that you fell silent, wondering what on
earth the clue to the mystery could be.

Yet when Hardy was in repose his face was
that of a seer. There was no doubt then, no need
to wonder what special privilege had admitted
him to so close a knowledge of his fellows. That
slight figure, with wisps of soft grey hair resting
on the collar of a tweed jacket, for his hair would
grow long at the back, blue-eyed, with a masterful nose that turned slightly from the straight,
whose raised and questioning eyebrows pushed
furrows up his forehead to the bald and shapely
head, had with his life work taken a place in

English literature with the few poets who could
stand near Shakespeare, and it was always easy
for me to feel that there was the very man. What
those people were told who asked for signs and
wonders we know. There the wonder was. There
sat the author of *The Dynasts*. And here, while
we are at Max Gate, is where we should acknowledge the debt we owe to Mrs. Hardy, for she ordained that he should be with us longer than his
frailty otherwise would have allowed.

While Hardy was with us his presence gave
dignity to our day. He was English, but because
he was the embodiment of qualities which are essentially of the tradition, and because he belonged
to the land as much as the heath and hawthorns
of Egdon, and the dateless barrows on the hill-
tops about his home, and the stones of Stinsford
church, he represented us in a way that Parlia-
ment cannot, and so he belongs to those in every
country who judge their neighbours by the best
their neighbours have done. There is more of the
salt of English life in the talk of the characters
who move in Hardy's novels, and more of the
English land in his scenes, than in all Hansard,
and in all the controversies and guide-books. If
strangers wish to know us, let them read Hardy;
but then, they will see only themselves in his

poems and stories. Hodge over his beer in a Dorset
inn, even when his drink has been aggrieved by
politicians and the press, sometimes drops a word
which is more convincing than the upshot of a
Parliamentary election. It is not recorded, except
in Hardy; and yet perhaps it may be the last word
on the subject, though it may take a century or
two for it to be repeated with effective emphasis.
Such words are like the flints in the soil; they
belong to it, and are sure to show when the earth
is stirred.

It is likely that if a company of English writers and critics were asked by a foreigner, who did
not know us, to what book he could turn for just
such a picture of England as would convince a
native that it was the origin of his bones, and his
nurture, and his destiny, those men might, in the
conventional way, consider first an exultant passage from Shakespeare. But I think that if one
of them were to mention the opening chapter of
The Return of the Native, then the others, after
a little surprise, would agree. There it is, at least
for the Englishman of today, in as memorable a
prose passage as there is in the language, that de-
scription of Egdon Heath at sunset. And it is not
in its sombreness, which might be of the dusk,
nor of some fancied impress there of things well

done which are forgotten; nor in the vague brightness of the last of the evening light in the sky, a light which might be the casual and accustomed sanction for what then is disappearing below into night; nor in the vague spaciousness of the heath; nor in those grotesque and dilated shadows which familiar objects assume in such a solitude at sundown to a sensitive traveller, shades that could be the nightly peopling of the scene by those who once knew it, but are gone. It is in such apprehensions, but there is something more, too; there is the entirely unreasonable surmise that we knew the heath before that gnarled thorn was young, before that white riband of road was new to it, before the barrows were on the ridges of the downs. I cannot believe this surmise is of pride in the continuity of the English. It is quite intimate. It has nothing to do with race, though perhaps it is not without a sense of fellowship.

Hardy himself never understood—or so it seemed to me, and, anyhow, I suppose such a modest man would not find it easy to believe it—that the people of his tales and the scenes in which they move are part of the life of the present English world; that the light from the country of his dreams falls across our reality and makes significant and so more easily endurable its garish-

271

ness. We have forgotten him as a great writer; his creation is part of our traditional landscape. We are to believe, on excellent authority, that we betray our provincialism if, when speaking of novels and novelists, we permit the mention of the more important English writers until after many Russians have been named. There is, says the voice of authority, a virtue called characterization, and the Russian novels have it, but the English in but an inferior way. Certainly this sounds difficult or wise. Yet suddenly we remember that there is more characterization in the last popular novel by a candid young lady than in all Greek drama. Where are we now? There is more fond characterization in Proust than in all Shakespeare. So what of it? Modern novels are full of characterization, and, good and bad together, they all soon die. Their candid revelations of character do not save them. So there is a chance, as the story called *Macbeth* still lives on, that we are deceived by what the fashion of the hour declares to be chiefly good in a story. We may as well be called provincial for it as anything else if we decline to displace the author of the Wessex novels. For it may still be true that the earth, and the sky, and the mystery of the force we call life, are more wonder-compelling than the oddi-

ties of any character we are likely to meet. The
earth was older as a character than Napoleon even
when he died, and it seems as though something
latent in the earth overbore him and all his
projects, whether or not that force was purposive,
whether or not there is an Immanent Will. The
earth was here before the earliest of man. What
word was given to it? We shall never learn that.
Perhaps the earth merely got going. Maybe com-
passion, which came with man, was as accidental
as the plesiosaurus or as falling downstairs.
There is no telling. We cannot learn what the
word was, if there were a word; yet if you read
again the last chapter of *The Woodlanders*; or if
on the top of Norcombe Hill with its "ancient
and decaying plantation of beeches" you watch
with Gabriel Oak while he revives a new-born
lamb by a fire in his hut, and looks to the stars
for the time, to see where the earth has swung
to in the heavens, then a conjecture of that
which transcends our brief life lets fall its shadow
over your reading. But the author gives it no
name. Not only is there no name for it, but the
creator of beauty is unaware of what he does.
Nevertheless, a conviction of continuity has come
to us through our reading, though the very stars
are passing. The conviction, it is true, may be only

they always flourished; and he is, too, the capacious barn of Bathsheba Everdene's farm, where the flocks were shorn, and where the sunlight on ancient walls which had witnessed centuries of such busy scenes, and the pungent fleece, were inseparable from the play of mind between Gabriel Oak and his charming but wayward young mistress. And Hardy is the High Street of Casterbridge and its corn-chandler, and a multitude of other men and women, and of familiar places so well accustomed to the ways of our fellows, and so unchanged in nature by the passage of time, that we feel those hamlets must be as enduring as the hills around them, and have foundations deeper than the roots of dynasties. There it is. Hardy suggests a ghostly virtue which chance and time cannot touch. Whatever that quality may be which suffuses our common words when a poet uses them, somehow it gives them an unaccustomed authority. The poet uses our common tongue to a new purpose, and we feel that after empires have fallen, still the poet and his people will be there. The next sunrise after the great downfall, the outlasting smoke is seen rising from cottage hearths, and a poet is still guarding the lamp which man once lighted.

Not so fast, though. For since Hardy's death a

special correspondent, as newspapers say, has been to Dorchester, and there he made the soothing discovery that Hardy is not read. The representative of a famous daily newspaper much more frequently perused than *The Dynasts*, journeyed all the way from London, and enquired of the young lady at the office desk of his hotel in Casterbridge —a quite natural and easy beginning for him— and without any fuss she admitted it. She cannot read Hardy. He is too sad. A tobacconist of the town agreed with her. They both named the authors they did read, though it is not for me to repeat their popular titles. The great daily paper thereupon announced next morning the important discovery in its headlines, "Hardy is too sad," on the word of those local authorities. It must be confessed that the hotel clerk, the tobacconist, and the journalist expressed a common opinion. I suppose we had better face the fact that, now Hardy has gone, there will be the usual attempts to diminish the significance of a poet's word to us. He will be too sad, and he will be unlike other writers, and several things will be wrong with him. The same type of mind, a common type, which never dared to look at the realities of war while they could be seen, nor would hear without a show of impatience the bleak advice of witnesses who knew, is quite willing now to applaud the romantic art of the cinema when it presents that war made vicariously out of dummies, fireworks, and heroics. A test of intelligence, we are told, is an ability to understand the implications of things. It is therefore clear that if we steadily decline to look at the realities of life, when they are painful, then our intelligence will be free from the application of a test so serious in its consequences; we shall not be found out. There will be no need for us to admit the truth, because we shall not know it. Hardy is too sad. Something else, and it is very important for us, is gained by our refusal to look at a saddening subject. We have escaped from more than one danger. If we deny Hardy, then we are exempt from contrast with a standard which would make us appear to be small. For he is not only sorrowful, he is great. Comparison with the great is unlucky. And if, being wise and great, he should be right, what are we? It is a simple instinct which makes us turn impatiently from the challenge of overshadowing figures such as Tolstoy and Hardy, and decline to look their way. We do not want to know. It was the work of the same sound instinct in us which took that terrible exposure of human follies, *Gulliver's Travels*, and made of it a gift book for children.

Yes, we can always put these challenging figures in a place where they will not be too noticeable, and we have ways of muffling their words. Their words might make a difference; and we do not want any difference. We prefer to be comfortable, and the taking of thought would not help. These men are disturbing. A common admission of the truth in their words would shatter so many of our ways and institutions that it is safer, we feel sure, to keep the teacher diminished and stultified. We know well, and without reasoning it out, what we are about. We know that a mind which could conceive *War and Peace*, or *The Dynasts*, must be wiser than our own, and must have access to knowledge beyond our range, and so we deny it; or, at the best, accept only so much of it as will not admit anxious criticism into our cheerful and haphazard ways of life. If we look to such men at all, we never fail to secure the satisfaction afforded by their feet of clay. Hardy gave us many volumes of verse; and yet, exclaimed a damaging critic recently, it is doubtful whether he wrote more than thirty good poems. No more than thirty? We are constrained to put the humble question: When is a poet not a poet? It might help us to understand the reason for the rarity of poetry if we knew how often the poet must perform the miraculous before we confess the miracle. For we remember that now we do not count the odes of Keats, nor refuse Coleridge because of his fragments. Had we not better be on our guard? It will be always easy for us to find reasons against admitting the light, because we guess at once, when threatened by the danger of illumination, that if darkness should go it would leave much disclosed that was quite well, while it was unseen.

While Hardy lived he justified the least of us, who serve humbly in Athena's temple. His presence did much to redeem this new age of mechanical science, in which the swarming Barbarians, who never doubt their appetites as men of civility question the difficulties of wisdom or falter at the exactions of art and learning, appear again to have taken control of the destinies of our cities. The Barbarians come this time, not in skins and with crude spears, but armed with the awful powers which engineering and chemical science have given them. We are compelled to submit to the discipline of their bristling tanks, and to the moulding of public opinion in the machinery of the popular newspaper press to those few forms of thought which money knows are the happiest; and to the reduction of our aspirations to simple and standardized desires that can be satisfied easily with public pomps and games, with music by mechanical apparatus, and a criticism of life by cinematograph drama. In such a world a great poet is unique, and definitely alien. His presence is a challenge to its powers. He keeps in heart his lesser brethren who oppose the things of the mind, though with no apparent success, to both the insolence of authority and the clamour of the market place.

It is the rare and isolated figure of the supreme artist which has always justified mankind and kept hope alive in us; for at times it is hard not to despair over our fellow men, who, with "loyal luckless hearts," as Hardy shows in *The Dynasts*, suffer our world, built of so much pain and labour, to be snatched at by gamblers to play with, and perhaps to lose, using its continents as boards for the chance of the dice. The poet justifies us because he himself is sublimated humanity. He embodies and exalts what is best in men and women, and for that very reason his poetry, because it expresses our better self, gives us the illusion that it has no practical virtue. Politics may be practical, but not poetry. Yet we cannot help

feeling a doubt that the Beatitudes may be beautifully impossible merely because we prefer the
cheerful sensations of the great oratory and great
doings by those statesmen and warriors who still
set the world by the ears. Those great men are
practical men—men of action, as the saying is—
and in the wreckage and distractions about us we
see a recent issue of their energetic and practical
minds. It has become a dismal joke that the only
man who came out of the last war with any credit
was Jesus of Nazareth.

Simple men and women everywhere are, to
some of us, better than any great statesman ever
expresses, even though they still look to him for
guidance. Common folk are much more akin to
the poet, who is, indeed, their true spokesman.
There is more in Hardy's work of what soldiers
have felt and said of war than in all the speeches
ever made by politicians, from Pitt to the last of
the famous leaders in war. Hardy the poet is ourselves, at our best. If there is a God to be known,
it is by looking to such a man. If the word is ever
made manifest in the flesh, and a purpose is ever
made plain in the chaos of time and chance, there
we have some clue to it. When the poet is cruci-
fied, then the multitude crucifies itself: the Pro-
Consul's guard may march back to the palace sat-

isfied that the road is cleared of the rabble. The poet is not a man apart, without aid for us in the manifold affairs of this busy world, an ineffective dreamer whose vision is unrelated to the things about us, and whose music is but æolian and of the empty air. He is the best that the crude realities have created. He is the outcome of all our doubts and strivings. He, if we but knew it, is the true culture and the crowning flower of the mud and compost out of which we all came. He, more than any other man, expresses what is the essential nature of the clay, and what it could be, and perhaps shall be.

❡ Out of Soundings *is set in Linotype Old Face.* *Format by A. W. Rushmore. Manufactured by The* *Haddon Craftsmen for the publisher*, Harper & Brothers.

Date Due

Demco 293-5